Jesus, Our Mentor and Model

Jesus, Our Mentor and Model

A Hero for Heroic Living

Harold Hazelip
Ken Durham

BAKER BOOK HOUSE
Grand Rapids, Michigan 49516

We lovingly dedicate this book to these heroes of faith who showed the way in following Jesus as Lord.

My parents,
Herbert and Maggie Hazelip

Harold Hazelip

My grandparents,
Ed and Madge Meixner

Ken Durham

Contents

Part 2
Ken Durham

Foreword

Every civilization, every nation, and perhaps every individual has had its heroes. Without such role models, the ideals we cherish never take on flesh and blood. And such disembodied ideals elude our grasp.

We all need heroes. Deep down, each of us wants to be a hero—one who leads . . . challenges . . . disturbs . . . exemplifies . . . calls us to sacrifice in order to excel.

Thomas Carlyle observed, "Show me the man you honor, and I will know what kind of man you are." Heroes—past and present—range from the admirable to the ridiculous.

The Bible describes Jesus as the authentic Hero! "For it was fitting that he, for whom and by whom all things exist, in bringing many sons to glory, should make the *pioneer* of their salvation perfect through suffering" (Heb. 2:10). ". . . looking to Jesus the *pioneer* and perfecter of our faith, who for the joy that was set before him endured the cross, despising the shame, and is seated at the right hand of the throne of God" (Heb. 12:2).

Jesus is the pioneer—the word might have been translated "author," "captain," "trailblazer," or "hero." He is the heroic God-man. As our brother who went before us, Jesus became our model and mentor for the truly heroic lifestyle.

9

We human beings instinctively have many needs. We encounter losses, suffer, search for meaning, struggle with guilt, shun responsibility, seek true relationships, and long to know God. We need goals, desire to communicate, work with relationships, and pursue peace of mind.

Did Jesus know these same needs? If so, how did he fulfill them? Where does the trail he blazed lead our lives? These are the questions we have addressed in this look at Jesus as the model for heroic living today.

Harold Hazelip
Ken Durham

PART

Harold Hazelip

1

Heroic Living
Living Above Life's Losses

A friend came home recently and discovered that intruders had been in his house. When he checked his belongings, the silver flatware was gone. Those knives, forks, and spoons were wedding gifts, the most expensive objects in the house. The police told him there was almost no chance that he would ever see the silver again.

We try to insulate ourselves from losses such as this. We insure our lives, our health, our homes, our cars, and all our personal possessions. Then we discover one day that the price we pay for having such treasures is that we ultimately experience loss. We lose our parents. We lose our spouse or a child. We lose our health. Some of us lose these things earlier than others, but in the end we all lose what we love.

How do we deal with life's losses? The great English writer C. S. Lewis did not marry until he was in his fifties. When he finally met Joy Davidman, he experienced all the exhilaration that we expect from young people who fall madly in love. Then, when they had been married only a few years, Joy began a long battle with the cancer that would finally lead to her death. Lewis told the story of his grief in a little book called *A Grief Observed*.

His warning to all of us who love is poignant: "Bereavement is a universal and integral part of our experience of love. It follows marriage as normally as marriage follows courtship or as autumn follows summer." Losing someone you love is not simply the interruption of a beautiful moment, Lewis says; it is the completion of an experience that begins with love.

Lewis first thought of his loss as a peculiar misfortune. Then he recognized that all lovers are finally torn apart. He recalled how Joy had said to him, "Even if we both died at exactly the same moment, as we lie here side by side, it would be just as much a separation as the one you're so afraid of."

Experiencing Losses

If you have lost someone who is very important to you, you know intellectually that you have much to be thankful for. A couple may live together for fifty years or longer, sharing a lifetime of happy memories of holidays, vacations, and quiet evenings at home. But a lifetime of happiness does not reduce the pain when one of them loses the other. A man who had lost his aged father explained, "It doesn't matter how long he lived. Separation is separation. I cannot stand the thought of being without him—forever."

We never quite get over the loss of a mate or a parent or a child. The pain may become less frequent, but it never goes away. Lewis (*A Grief Observed*, New York, Bantam, 1963) commented,

> To say the patient is getting over it after an operation for appendicitis is one thing; after he's had his leg off it is quite another. After that operation either the wounded stump heals or the man dies. If it heals, the fierce, continuous pain will stop. Presently he will get back his strength and be able to stump about on his wooden leg. . . . But he will have recurrent pains in the stump all his life, and perhaps pretty bad ones; and he will always be a one-legged man. There will be hardly any moment when he forgets it. Bathing, dressing, sitting down and getting up again, even lying in bed, will all

be different. His whole way of life will be changed. All sorts of pleasures and activities that he once took for granted will have to be simply written off (p. 61).

There is some comfort in knowing that we do not simply "get over it" when we lose a loved one. Our relationship was so deep that we seem to have no memories and no history without that special person. Only when people do not mean much to us can we forget them easily.

This is not only true when we lose someone we love. Other losses hurt too. Beethoven recognized early in life that he was losing his hearing. He never "got over" his loss, since he would never again enjoy his own music.

All of us sooner or later will face the moment when we can no longer do what we once did. The ordinary things that gave us delight—seeing, walking, speaking, hearing—are taken from us once and for all. When this happens it shakes us to the core and makes us wonder how we can get any joy out of life when the things that brought such pleasure have been taken from us.

Biblical Characters Suffered Losses

Religious people may be shaken more than anyone when they suffer a deep loss. Perhaps we think our faith will bring a guarantee against suffering. But we do not have to read far in the Bible to recognize the losses, the pain, and the tears in the lives of men and women of faith.

Think of the agony of Jacob when his sons led him to believe that Joseph had been killed. Jacob said, ". . . in mourning will I go down to the grave to my son . . ." (Gen. 37:35, NIV).

King David later became Israel's greatest hero. Yet he brought tragedy on himself by his own actions. He lost one child after another. One died in infancy. One son killed his half-brother. One died while leading a rebellion against his father. Another died in a struggle for the throne as King David himself lay dying.

The Old Testament is filled with cries of despair over losses that had to be borne. The psalmist cried out in unforgettable words, "My God, my God, why hast thou forsaken me?"; and then he asked, "Why art thou so far from helping me, from the words of my groaning? O my God, I cry by day, but thou dost not answer; and by night, but find no rest" (Ps. 22:1–2). Those words became Jesus' cry from the cross.

Another cry came from Christianity's greatest missionary. We do not know the nature of Paul's thorn-in-the-flesh (2 Cor. 12:7), but it appears to have been a debilitating illness. Whatever it was, it was a loss that was to remain with him the rest of his life. It was not something like a sprained ankle that he would soon get over. He had to live with it.

Jesus knew the pain of losing. The stories he told often centered on the experience of losing. Luke 15 relates three such examples. A shepherd lost one of his sheep, and he trudged through the hills and ravines until he found it. A woman lost one of her ten coins, and she turned the house upside down until she found it. A father lost one of his two sons when the younger one wanted to be free. There was little the father could do to stop him; he could only grieve over his wayward boy.

These stories of Jesus all have happy endings. What was lost was recovered. A celebration followed in each case. But for us it often seems that no celebration is in sight. The loved ones who have been taken from us will not return. The gifts and abilities we once had are gone, and they will never return. How do we go on living? We can learn from the lives of those who refused to quit.

There is a line in Paul's letter to the Romans that lets us see the way he faced his losses. The apostle wrote, ". . . we rejoice in our sufferings, knowing that suffering produces endurance, and endurance produces character, and character produces hope" (Rom. 5:3–4). Paul indicates that Christians are not insulated from suffering and loss. Each day brings its tests. But each test that is passed becomes a victory in a growth process that goes on until the very end of life.

Growing Above Our Losses

Four suggestions may help us to live above life's losses. First, we should not be ashamed of the grief that leads us to complain about our loss. Our first step in living above our loss may be to admit that we have been hurt deeply. Shakespeare said it well in Macbeth: "Give sorrow words; the grief that does not speak/Whispers the o'er-fraught heart and bids it break." It is perfectly normal to talk about the anger, the hurt, the depression, we feel.

Many of the Psalms are helpful at this point because they show us that it is not unthinkable to express our hurt and even our anger. We may be shocked to read the psalmist's cry of despair and even more amazed to read the same words on the lips of Jesus: "My God, my God, why hast thou forsaken me?" But the psalmist did take his complaint to God, keeping the conversation with him open.

It is well that such words are in the Bible. They record the experiences of real people—men and women who refused to give up or resign themselves to their condition. What we want to avoid at all costs is the temptation to give up on life.

Second, part of our growth process will come through focusing our attention on something beyond our own condition. Athletes who are caught up in the goal of winning a game seem to be oblivious to pain from their injuries.

Doctors Wayne and Charles Oates, in *People in Pain*, tell the story of Dr. John Bonica who established the University of Washington Medical Center's Clinical Pain Service some twenty years ago. In this center specialists from eight to ten different areas combine their efforts to unravel the mystery of pain syndromes. The inspiration for this program came from its founder, who lives in constant pain. At the age of sixty-seven, Bonica says that only his intense involvement in his work keeps him from being "a completely disabled guy." If he allowed himself to think only of his losses, he could not go on. But his purpose in life—to help suffering people—lifts him above the tyranny of pain and gives him energy.

Third, our losses must be faced and integrated into our lives. When Beethoven's famous "Ode to Joy" was first performed before a German audience, the melody brought great applause. But Beethoven could hear it only in his imagination.

When he was first diagnosed as facing deafness, Beethoven reacted with angry outbursts. He wrote to a friend, "Your Beethoven is most unhappy and at strife with nature and the Creator." At first he withdrew from others and refused to tell them of his problem. But he knew he could never be happy if he did not compose music. Slowly he began to integrate the illness into his life.

We do not know what Beethoven would have been like without his illness, but we do know that his loss did not stop him. He grew from the point where he thought his purpose in life was at an end to the place where he could work above his illness to become one of the world's greatest composers. Katherine Mansfield wrote in her journal:

> I should like this to be accepted as my confession. There is no limit to human suffering. When one thinks: "Now I have touched the bottom of the sea—now I can go no deeper," one goes deeper. . . . But I do not want to die without leaving a record of my belief that it can be overcome. . . . What must one do? One must submit. Do not resist. Take it. Be overwhelmed. Accept it fully. Make it part of your life.

Our growth process toward living above life's losses will take place when we use those losses to benefit other people. Paul wrote to the Corinthians, "Blessed be the God and Father of our Lord Jesus Christ, the Father of mercies and God of all comfort, who comforts us in all our affliction, so that we may be able to comfort those who are in any affliction, with the comfort with which we ourselves are comforted by God" (2 Cor. 1:3–4).

A certain lady lived in constant pain for twenty of her forty-six years. She never believed that she deserved her loss of good health. At times she got some comfort from her freedom to lay her burden before God, accompanied by a complaint. But even more comfort came from the belief that she could use her suffering to help others. She made herself available to other sufferers, to share her own experience with them. She met with ministers to help them understand how to help those who were suffering. This woman's greatest comfort came from the belief that her suffering had some value for her own children. She had two teenagers—a boy and a girl. She believed they were less selfish, more compassionate, and more able to help other people because of living with her through her suffering. She had grown to see that some good could come from her loss of health.

To grow above our losses, we must recognize that we cannot always expect happy endings. We have to live with our losses and integrate them into our lives. But this is not the end of the story. The Christian hope is that one day there will be a happy ending, and that God is preparing us for it now. Once again Paul's words are helpful: "For this slight momentary affliction is preparing us for an eternal weight of glory beyond all comparison" (2 Cor. 4:17).

2

Heroic Struggle
Keeping Faith in a Cruel World

Have you noticed how quickly little children develop a sense of order and fair play? One of the first complete sentences a child makes is: "It isn't fair!" Children have a keen sense of justice. Everything—toys and playthings, rewards and punishment—is supposed to be measured and evenly distributed.

We never lose this conviction that the world should be fair, that we should get what we deserve. Work hard, pay your bills, go to church, and the world should treat you right—you get the home in the suburbs, two cars in the garage, and children you can be proud of. On the other hand, calamity should strike those who live the wrong way.

That is how the world is supposed to be. That is how it would have been if *we* had created the world, we say. But we did not create the world. God did. And we soon recognize that this world offends our sense of fairness. Good people get struck down at the peak of their careers. Earthquakes and natural disasters hit churches and hospitals and innocent people everywhere.

We have all seen our share of such tragedies. We have talked to bereaved parents, widows, and friends. They almost always ask, "Why?" What they really mean is, "Why

21

would a powerful and loving God allow this? It just isn't fair." It is not an easy question to answer.

Chaim Potok's latest novel, *Davita's Harp,* tells of an idealistic young journalist who left his wife and child to cover the Spanish Civil War. He knew that being a war correspondent was dangerous, but to him it was a sacred cause. He and his wife were dedicated Communists; they saw the victory of Fascism as a disaster. Michael, the young journalist, was killed in the town of Guernica in an air raid. His wife Hannah grieved, but she never asked about God. She had given up on God in her youth, when she felt abandoned during the persecutions of Jews in her native Poland.

In the novel, Hannah tries to explain these tragedies to ten-year-old Davita, their daughter. She could only say, "It has been a bad century." She said that fifty years ago, but we can still say that it has been a bad century. Innocent people are slaughtered in airports and on the streets for no other reason than that they were in the wrong place at the wrong time.

Why Is God Silent?

Anyone who has given up on God, like Davita's mother, may not raise questions in the face of suffering. Perhaps not many of us have given up on God, but there are those who ask why God seems silent, why a merciful God sits idly by, while unfair tragedy takes its toll. C. S. Lewis reports in *A Grief Observed* a very angry notation in his journal when he actually accused God of his wife's death.

Instead of blaming their troubles on God, others simply ask why they have been abandoned by God. Elijah taunted the prophets of Baal when their god did not answer: ". . . either he is musing . . . or he is on a journey, or perhaps he is asleep and must be awakened" (1 Kings 18:27). And God sometimes seems silent when we need him most.

Shortly after World War II, Wilhelm Borchert, a German playwright, wrote a gripping play entitled *The Man Outside.* The chief character came home from a prison camp, only to discover there was no one to welcome him. His wife had married someone else, and his parents had been killed in the war. His employer did not want to see him, and his friends would have nothing to do with him. The play ended with the haunting words, "Where is the old man named God? Why doesn't he speak up? Why is he silent? Is there no answer?"

Our affluence may obscure our need for God. When we are surrounded by comforts and things, when we seem in control of our own destiny, God may seem irrelevant to us. Then the illusion that we can take care of ourselves is stripped away by disease or death. We discover that we are not very different from the people centuries ago who cried out for God in their moments of despair.

The Bible portrays men and women who agonized over the silence of God. The frankness of the biblical writers who recorded their struggles with their faith in God is striking. The honesty of the Psalms, for example, is remarkable. The words of Psalm 22:1–2, quoted by Jesus on the cross, have been repeated through the centuries:

> My God, my God, why hast thou forsaken me?
> Why art thou so far from helping me, from the words of my
> groaning?
> O my God, I cry by day, but thou dost not answer;
> and by night, but find no rest.

Evildoers were oppressing the psalmist. His trust in God had not protected him from disaster.

The author of Psalm 44 recalled stories he had heard about the power and goodness of God. Then he complained:

> Yet thou hast cast us off and abased us
> and hast not gone out with our armies. . . .
> Thou hast made us like sheep for slaughter,
> and hast scattered us among the nations. . . .
> Thou hast made us the taunt of our neighbors,
> the derision and scorn of those about us (vv. 9, 11, 13).

And then he begged God to awaken and remember his people:

Rouse thyself! Why sleepest thou, O Lord?
Awake! Do not cast us off for ever!
Why dost thou hide thy face?
Why dost thou forget our affliction and oppression? (vv.
   23–24).

One of the most unforgettable passages in the Book of Job
is Job's complaint against God in chapter 23. Job had lost his
family and had been abandoned by his friends. Job felt that
God had abandoned him, and he said:

Oh, that I knew where I might find him,
   that I might come even to his seat!
I would lay my case before him
   and fill my mouth with arguments (vv. 3–4).

Job wished for an umpire to referee his case with God.
Then he cried:

Behold, I go forward, but he is not there;
and backward, but I cannot perceive him;
on the left hand I seek him, but I cannot behold him;
I turn to the right hand, but I cannot see him (vv. 8–9).

The Bible offers us a long record of people who believed in
God but found his ways hidden from their understanding. In
the words of the Book of Isaiah, "Truly, thou art a God who
hidest thyself, O God of Israel, the Savior" (Isa. 45:15).

God on the Cross

Why is God so silent when we need him most? I have to
admit that I find all of the explanations a bit inadequate. We
do not know why there must be Guernicas and Hiroshimas
or why little children die, though some of the standard explanations are helpful as we search for answers.

"I can explain all of the poems that ever were invented,"
said Humpty Dumpty, "and a good many that haven't been

invented just yet." Lewis Carroll, the author of *Alice in Wonderland*, was using a bit of satire to deal with the modern world. We recognize Humpty Dumpty as "the great explainer."

From early childhood we are bombarded with explanations of everything from the solar system to the process of photosynthesis. But can everything be explained?

In another scene Alice made this very point. "Explain yourself," said the Caterpillar. "I can't explain myself, I am afraid, sir," said Alice. Neither can you or I. The most crucial aspects of our lives—why we exist and what we are supposed to be—are not things that can be explained like the workings of a clock. Love cannot be explained. God cannot be explained. And God's ways cannot be explained.

From our vantage point, we can look at only one side of the tapestry; from this one side, we cannot see the beautiful work God is weaving. In Paul's words, our sufferings are nothing compared to the future glory. And suffering sometimes develops character and builds our faith.

But these are only partial answers. Job cried out for an explanation, but the book ends without one. After all our attempts to understand, we are left with the words of Isaiah: "For my thoughts are not your thoughts, neither are your ways my ways, says the LORD" (Isa. 55:8).

The Bible does not offer explanations for our sufferings. It offers something else. These are Paul's words in Romans:

What then shall we say to this? If God is for us, who is against us? He who did not spare his own Son but gave him up for us all, will he not also give us all things with him? . . . Who shall separate us from the love of Christ? Shall tribulation, or distress, or persecution, or famine, or nakedness, or peril, or sword? . . . No, in all these things we are more than conquerors through him who loved us. For I am sure that neither death, nor life, nor angels, nor principalities, nor things present, nor things to come, nor powers, nor height, nor depth, nor anything else in all creation, will be able to separate us from the love of God in Christ Jesus our Lord (Rom. 8:31–32, 35, 37–39).

Paul had seen his share of suffering. He knew that good people are sometimes hungry, while evil men and women seem to flourish in their immorality. But Paul did not cry out for an umpire, as Job did. He did not complain that God is hidden, as Isaiah did. Paul knew God's love in Jesus Christ. God gave his very best for us.

The Old Testament has the story of Abraham, who was asked by God to take his son Isaac up Mount Moriah to be sacrificed. Isaac was the child of Abraham's old age, the child he had prayed and waited for. Though the story ends with God intervening to protect Isaac, it describes in vivid detail Abraham's willingness to give up his only son for God's sake. This, Paul said, is what God did in giving up Christ for us. He is not sitting in his heaven aloof from our pain.

New Testament writers never explain our suffering, but they are so overwhelmed by the story of the cross that they never seem to doubt the love of God. In the presence of hardship or when they were destitute, the writers continued to say, "We have been loved." "For God so loved the world that he gave his only Son," John said (John 3:16). Paul added, ". . . while we were yet sinners Christ died for us" (Rom. 5:8).

Help for the Struggle

We cannot fully explain our suffering. But when people ask for a word from God in the midst of their pain, there are some considerations that help.

First, no tragedy is to be taken as a sign that God has rejected you. Paul saw in front of him persecution, hardship, and death. Yet behind the scenes he saw the love of God in Christ. The crucifixion of Jesus is our assurance that God will not reject us. He loved us that much!

Second, though we may not know how another feels, since we have not shared their grief, the very center of Christian faith is the God who feels our pain. The cross is the permanent reminder that God can grieve with us and suffer when we suffer. He agonizes when people die prematurely and when they are eaten away with disease. He mourns when human beings lose those dear to them.

Third, our present pain is not the end of the story. God did not spare his own Son. He has come too far with us to abandon us now. This is why Paul could look at death itself and say, "If God is for us, who is against us? He who did not spare his own Son but gave him up for us all, will he not also give us all things with him?" (Rom. 8:32). When everything seems to indicate that our situation is hopeless, the story of the cross and the resurrection shows that God is not finished with his work. The cross is God's eternal sign that he cares.

Fourth, we are not alone in our suffering! The community of Christians cares because Christ has taught us to care. Christians may not come with explanations, as Job's comforters did, but they come with the love that God has poured out on them. "Rejoice with those who rejoice," Paul wrote, "weep with those who weep" (Rom. 12:15). "If one member suffers, all suffer together . . ." (1 Cor. 12:26).

Perhaps the final word is that we do not know what good may come from our suffering. But the Bible says, "We know that in everything God works for good with those who love him . . ." (Rom. 8:28). Someday, God will complete the work he began when he gave up his only Son. Meanwhile, he helps us to struggle heroically in a world that often seems cruel.

3

Heroic Purpose
Doing Something Meaningful with Our Lives

Over 150 years ago a French historian named Alexis de Tocqueville visited the United States. One of the things that impressed him most in the Americans he met was their "individualism." Tocqueville wrote, "There are more and more people who, though neither rich nor powerful enough to have much hold over others, have gained or kept enough wealth and understanding to look after their own needs. Such folk owe no man anything and hardly expect anything from anybody."

Thomas Jefferson wrote in our Declaration of Independence that every individual is endowed by his creator with the "unalienable right" to "life, liberty, and the pursuit of happiness." When we recall our early American heroes, we admire their self-reliance, their rugged individualism. We grew up learning of Benjamin Franklin, the self-made man, and Abraham Lincoln, who overcame every obstacle in pursuit of a great destiny.

But there is another side to this individualism. Tocqueville was concerned that it might lead us to think only of ourselves and our own pursuits. What happens when we begin to live only for ourselves? The individualism we ad-

29

mire can turn into a selfishness that has little interest in others.

This is a danger in our culture's current obsession with "self-fulfillment." A university student in Texas recently described his high-school career as the pursuit of one identity after another. During his freshman year, he took on the identity of a cowboy and dressed accordingly. During his sophomore year, he took on the identity and appearance of a motorcycle gang member. In his junior year, he adopted the unusual clothing and hairstyle of the "new wave." And, in his senior year, he took on the button-down look of a "preppie" on his way to college. Each year he had a new identity, complete with its own costume, its own peer group, and its own values.

His story reminds me of Homer's ancient description of Proteus, the sea god. Homer said that Proteus could "assume all manner of shapes of all things that move upon the earth, and of water, and of wondrous blazing fire." This mythical figure has led modern writers to speak of "the Protean man." The Protean man is always changing shapes, playing whatever part is assigned to him or seems expedient.

This kind of conduct is not limited to adolescents. One of the Watergate conspirators later said that the whole experience had been one exercise in role playing. The only way to survive was to play the part that was assigned. If one played the role well, this might lead to a bigger role and a chance to get to the top and "be somebody!"

This may be the reason we are willing to play certain roles and switch identities. We want to be someone important. The thirst for individual achievement runs deeply in our American character. Long ago Walt Whitman wrote the poem "Song of Myself":

> Afoot and light-hearted I take to the open road,
> Healthy, free, the world before me,
> The long brown path before me, leading wherever I choose.

Whitman believed the individual finds fulfillment when he ignores tradition and society and makes his own choices.

Finding Ourselves

It is an old theme: we must find ourselves! We are not to be controlled by the concerns of others. There are two very serious problems with this approach to "finding ourselves."

First, can anyone imagine finding personal fulfillment that does not include others who mean very much to us? What we hear constantly today is that the choice of friends, loved ones, and careers should be subject to immediate cancellation. Marriage must be open-ended, since "till death do us part" may impede the fulfillment of the individual. All other relationships—friendships, parent-child and other family bonds, and professional ties—must be treated in the same way. They can be discarded as we "keep our options open" in hope of finding ourselves. Does anyone seriously believe this kind of self-centeredness can produce happiness and fulfillment?

There is a second problem with this obsession for self-fulfillment. If we are merely chameleons and constantly changing our coloration in order to succeed, where are the core values in our lives? Robert Bellah and a team of sociologists recently described the mood of Americans in their book *Habits of the Heart*. They described a man who was so caught up in climbing the corporate ladder that he neglected his family and was later divorced. He remarried, determined not to repeat his same mistakes. In his second marriage he devoted the time to be a good husband and father. But, according to the authors, this new choice was only a matter of preference. He chose his family over his work this time, not because it was right, but because it gave him more satisfaction.

Bellah and his associates interviewed a large number of Americans to learn something about the national character today. They discovered a widespread conviction that each person creates his or her own moral world. Mark Twain is given credit for the description of the moral act as "something you feel good after" and the immoral act as "something you feel bad after." When we most want, it seems, is something that makes us feel good. Yet we are not sure what goals in life are really worth pursuing.

At the end of Arthur Miller's play *The Death of a Salesman*, one of Willie Loman's sons says of him, "He never really knew who he was." Willie's entire life of looking out for Number One had ended in suicide. The Protean man, who always changes his shape in order to succeed, is following a blind alley. What he needs most is a compass, a set of values, a goal in life to guide his choices.

A Whole New World

If we were to try to summarize the story of Jesus, there would be no better way than to say, "One died for all." These were Paul's words in his second letter to the Corinthians: "For the love of Christ controls us, because we are convinced that one has died for all; therefore all have died" (2 Cor. 5:14).

The Bible has many ways of saying this. When Paul reflected on the message he had proclaimed in Corinth he wrote, ". . . Christ died for our sins in accordance with the scriptures" (1 Cor. 15:3). To the Romans he said, "While we were yet helpless, at the right time Christ died for the ungodly. . . . But God shows his love for us in that while we were yet sinners Christ died for us" (Rom. 5:6, 8). He spoke to the Galatians about the One who "loved me and gave himself for me" (Gal. 2:20). Whenever Paul thought of the death of Jesus, he added the words, "for our sins . . . for us . . . for me."

Those words were more than a piece of history or doctrine for Paul. They were his compass. They shaped the kind of man he was. Far from being a Protean man who changed his shape to fit the situation, Paul's life was shaped by Jesus' self-giving example. He wrote, "If anyone is in Christ, it is a whole new world" (2 Cor. 5:17, NEB). That is, the Christian sees the world in a different way. He marches to the sound of a different drummer.

Dr. Stanley Hauerwas has written a book titled *Vision and Virtue*. In it he argues that character is the basis for making moral decisions. And character is a moral orientation that comes from our vision of what is good. This thing called "character" is what is lacking when people are willing to discard all relationships in order to succeed.

In the paragraphs of Scripture cited above, Paul was saying that the story of the man who died on the cross had forever shaped his identity and given him his character. And so Paul knew who he was. He was quite willing to live for others, to suffer sleepless nights and exhaustion for the sake of others. He could forget personal advancement in order to serve others.

Paul used vivid language to tell us why he would pour out his life for others: ". . . the love of Christ controls us" (2 Cor. 5:14). The word for "control" was the term commonly used for a prisoner who had been taken into custody. The love of Christ had taken Paul captive. Paul looked and acted differently because he had experienced the love of Christ.

A Goal Beyond Ourselves

Nothing is more important in making our lives worth living than to live for some cause that is greater than ourselves. Someone has spoken of "the poverty of affluence." We have so many material things, but what we are missing is that delight in being captured, in losing ourselves, for the sake of something important. Viktor Frankl wrote in his book *The Unheard Cry for Meaning:* "The affluent society has given vast segments of population the means, but people cannot see an end, a meaning to live for. In addition, we are living in a leisure society; ever more people have ever more time to spend, but nothing meaningful on which to spend it."

Dr. Frankl tells of a letter he received from a family doctor: "For half a year my very dear father was seriously ill with cancer. The last three months of his life he lived in my house—looked after by my beloved wife and myself. What I really want to tell you is that those three months were the most blessed times in the lives of my wife and me. . . . Until his last evening I kept telling him how happy we were that we could experience this close contact for those last weeks, and how poor we would have been if he had just died from a heart attack lasting just a few seconds." Ours may not be the life we would choose, but the inconvenience is worthwhile if we are caught up in something greater than ourselves!

Henry David Thoreau wrote, "If a man does not keep pace with his companions, it is because he hears a different drummer. Let him step to the music which he hears, however measured or far away." As Paul described the great cause he had come to live for, he wrote, "And he died for all, that those who live might live no longer for themselves but for him who for their sake died and was raised" (2 Cor. 5:15). We march to the sound of a different drummer: the story of the One who died for all. Jesus was Paul's hero!

Many people have been captured by that story. Think of the missionary in Africa, the volunteer in the diseased slums of Calcutta. And there are many others who are closer to home. The father whose schedule is determined by the needs of his retarded child, not by his own ambition. People with talent and imagination who have chosen to serve Christ in the decaying city rather than in more comfortable surroundings. Professional people—doctors and lawyers—who devote a substantial amount of their time serving those who cannot pay the normal fees.

Willie Loman did not know who he was because he had never found something bigger than himself to capture his imagination. What Christians have found is a goal that has led us captive. If we are bored or looking for a new and more meaningful life, Christ can introduce us to a whole new world. We discover ourselves when we discover the joy of giving ourselves for others.

4

Heroic Conscience
Coping with Guilt

Garrison Keillor had one of the characters in his humorous book *Lake Wobegon Days* write his own "ninety-five theses" to his parents—a list of all the things his parents had done to ruin his life. Their voices—the voices from his childhood—still rang in his head.

What feelings did his parents arouse in this man? "Guilt," he said. "Guilt as a child, then anger at you for filling me with guilt, then guilt at the anger. Then I tried to relieve that guilt by presenting you with a wonderful trip to Los Angeles." But even this did no good because the parents could not accept the trip. And so he still felt guilty.

What good is guilt? A chapter title in a recent book offering prescriptions for happiness read: "The Useless Emotions: Guilt and Worry." Is something wrong with us when we feel guilty? Should we feel guilty about feeling guilty?

Many people today would like to abolish guilt. One of the most frequent clichés one hears is, "Don't lay a guilt trip on me." Guilt is a holdover from the Middle Ages. Or from the time of Hester Prynne, the unfortunate girl of Nathaniel Hawthorne's *The Scarlet Letter*. We are told to accept ourselves as we are and that it is useless to feel guilty.

Guilt Is Here to Stay

Anyone who counsels with others soon finds many people
with a severe sense of guilt. We may want nothing more
than to tell them that they do not need to feel guilty about a
particular situation. There is the teenager who cannot con-
vince himself that he was not the cause of his parents' divorce. There is the young couple who decides when their
child is born with a birth defect, "God must be punishing us
for something." A family member is killed in an automobile
accident and everyone says, "If only we had warned him not
to take that route. . . ."

There is such a thing as useless guilt. We see it when we
punish ourselves unnecessarily for things that were outside
our control.

But, at another level, every one of us should feel guilty
because we *are* guilty. In the words of Scripture: ". . . all have
sinned and fall short of the glory of God" (Rom. 3:23). The
Bible pronounces judgment on all of us—the churchgoers,
the philanthropists, the dedicated physicians and mission-
aries, as well as the sinners we can readily identify.

Someone has said that "guilt represents the noblest and
most painful of struggles. It is between us and ourselves."
Feeling guilty tells us that we have failed our own ideals.
Guilt places us before an invisible tribunal, which measures
our offense and tells us how serious it really is.

A conscientious doctor failed to notice a tiny speck on a
CAT scan. The speck turned out to be a malignant tumor.
Had he noticed it earlier, he might have taken measures that
would have saved a life. But he had overlooked it. Now he
must face the patient with the news, and he must face himself. Why had he missed the tumor? Had he been preoccupied that day with his own concerns or those of other
patients? Had he been in too much of a hurry? He received
the guilty verdict from himself.

Many parents are overcome with guilt because their work
as parents looks like failure. "Where did we go wrong?" they

ask. Most of these parents are good people. They have been conscientious about their task. Now the father (or mother) wonders, "Did I not spend enough time with my children? Was I too preoccupied with my own career?"

We do become so caught up in our own pursuits that we fail to live up to our ideals. We know that our aged parents have been lonely for years. But the parents do not ask for help, and the years go by. Then it dawns on us that we have not taken time for the things that matter most.

Guilt hits us hard because it always comes after it seems too late to rectify what went wrong. We cannot go back and do our parenting again. We cannot unwind the years and be the kind of children we should have been. We cannot undo our wrong deeds as marriage partners. So we go on carrying the baggage of the past with us.

One of Jane Austen's most endearing heroines, Emma Woodhouse, was chastised one day by Mr. Knightley for being unkind to a boring and talkative elderly woman. "How could you be so insolent in your wit to a woman of her character, age, and situation?" he asked. "Emma, I had not thought it possible."

Emma blushed and tried to laugh it off, but before she had the opportunity, Mr. Knightley left. Her frustration at not being able to acknowledge her wrongdoing left her feeling progressively more guilty:

> Never had she felt so agitated, mortified, grieved at any circumstances in her life. . . . The truth of his representation there was no denying. She felt it at her heart. How could she have been so brutal, so cruel, to Miss Bates? . . . Time did not compose her. As she reflected more, she seemed to feel it more.

Her own private tribunal told her that she had failed.

Anton Chekhov has a story of a young woman named Olga, who was married to a kind, good husband. Earlier in their marriage she had betrayed him. Then Chekhov described a scene where her husband lay dying of diphtheria while Olga watched in misery, recalling her betrayal. Chekhov wrote:

> Olga no longer thought of the moonlit Volga night, the romance of life in the peasant's hut. She remembered only that from caprice and selfishness she had smeared herself from head to feet with something vile and sticky which no washing could wash away.

Shakespeare immortalized this same feeling when he had Lady Macbeth cry out, "Out, damned spot! out, I say! . . . Will these hands ne'er be clean?"

We may try very hard to ignore our guilt by making excuses. Our failures are someone else's fault, we say. We are only the product of our heredity or our environment. We blame our parents or society. Like Adam and Eve in the garden, we become adept at shifting the blame to someone else. But we soon discover that it is not easy to get rid of guilt and shame.

When we were children, many of us were taught that there are sins of commission and sins of omission. This distinction still makes sense. We have all done things we cannot undo and said things we cannot "unsay." Then there are the things we simply neglected to do. We were not as good husbands or wives, parents or children, as we would have liked to be. And our inner tribunal tells us so.

There is no more graphic reminder anywhere than Paul's confession of his own failures: "I do not understand my own actions," he wrote in Romans. "For I do not do what I want, but I do the very thing I hate. . . . I can will what is right, but I cannot do it. For I do not do the good I want, but the evil I do not want is what I do" (Rom. 7:15, 18b–19). Despite our good intentions, we fail to be what we want to be.

What Happens to Guilt?

We do not like feeling guilty. But at least the feeling of guilt tells us that we still have standards. It is as important to our well-being to feel guilt as it is to feel pain. In each case, the feeling tells us to move away from danger and protects us from destroying ourselves. But how shall we deal with our guilt?

Guilt can be a good thing if we handle it with care. Frederick Buechner has written:

> It is about as hard to absolve yourself of your own guilt as it is to sit in your own lap. Wrongdoing sparks guilt sparks wrongdoing *ad nauseam*, and we disguise the grim process from both ourselves and everybody else. In order to break the circuit we need somebody before whom we can put aside the disguise, trusting that when he sees us for what we fully are, he won't run away screaming with, if nothing worse, laughter.

Luke 7:36–50 tells the story of a woman who apparently knew she was guilty and that only someone else could give her the forgiveness and strength to rebuild her life. Luke only identifies the woman as "a sinner." He does not tell us the source of her guilt, but it was intense.

This woman came to a dinner party where Jesus was. She had with her an expensive jar of ointment. She was so overcome in his presence that she washed the feet of Jesus with her tears. Then she wiped his feet with her own hair and anointed his feet with the ointment. It was a disgrace in that culture for a woman to let her hair down in public. Apparently she was so ashamed of herself that it no longer mattered if she disgraced herself a bit more. She was helpless—trapped with a past she hated, stuck with a reputation that hurt her, carrying around a guilt she could not remove.

She could have done what many of us do with our guilt. She could have shifted the blame to others: to society, to her family, to economic conditions that had pushed her into her own disgrace. She could have lashed out in anger at the smug indifference of the good people who would not accept her as she was. Instead, she knew she was guilty, and her guilt sent her looking for a new life.

Some of us want forgiveness while we remain as we are, a forgiveness that will allow us to go on with our wrongdoing. This was not the kind of desire that brought this woman to Christ at the dinner party. She came in tears. Without a deep sense of guilt, she would not have moved to put her life back together again.

Those who stood by could only see in her behavior the proof that she had ruined her life. But what Jesus saw was her repentance. And so he said, "Your sins are forgiven." It was his way of saying, "You can escape this vicious circle. God is willing to accept you. You can believe in yourself because I believe in you."

The heart of the Christian message is: "You cannot take away your own guilt, but God can release you from your own disgust with yourself. God will accept you." Jesus said it when he sat down to eat with tax collectors and prostitutes. They all hated themselves. When Jesus said to Zacchaeus, "I'm going to your house today," he was saying, "God is willing to accept you." It took someone else to take the guilt away, and Jesus was the One who liberated people from their past.

When we see these characters who came to Jesus with their guilt, we recognize something of ourselves. We, too, have not been what we should have been. We see in those gospel stories all of us who feel trapped in a life we hate. And his word to all of us is: "God loves you. He will accept you." This is why Christians call the story of Jesus "good news." Our guilt can be taken away.

But these stories about sinners who came to Jesus leave us hanging. We want to know what happened next! Where did this sinful woman go the next day? And the week after that? Did she return to the same old lifestyle and then feel all the more guilty because she could not improve herself? We like to think that she was never the same again, that her guilt brought her to have the radical surgery on her life that changed her forever.

We know for a fact that this is what Jesus intended. He did not forgive her so that she could return to a disgusting life. He forgave her so that she could change directions.

Ways to Handle Guilt

Our guilt may be destructive, but it may also be a good thing. It may be like the pain that runs through our bodies, telling us that something is wrong and that we need to give it our attention and correct the problem. Pain can be a very good thing if we treat it correctly. Three guidelines will help us deal with the pain of our guilt.

First, we must not ignore our guilt. We must have the courage to admit it. As we examine our lives to see why we are feeling guilty, we will recognize the truth about ourselves. No one should indulge in the self-deception that his or her life is unblemished.

Second, we must see the One who can do something about our guilt. We come to recognize, as the sinful woman did, that we cannot atone for our guilt. There is Jesus—he who still loves us and will accept us. We must believe it! Believe that he believes in us! In this way, the burden can be lifted. We simply find the courage to repent of our wrongdoing and submit our will to God's will.

Third, when we have been forgiven of our guilt, we must know that we cannot go on living as we once did. We cannot expect God to forgive us of our guilt if we are unwilling to change. We dare not abuse his love. He will give us the strength to overcome if we will make the effort to change the pattern of life that has made us guilty in the first place.

Those of us who have been Christians for a very long time still discover things about ourselves that we do not like very much. We make mistakes as husbands and fathers and wives and mothers. But we have discovered in Christ the One who understands, who forgives, and who gives us new strength to try again.

5

Heroic Maturity
Taking Responsibility for Our Lives

One of the great advances in our time is that we have discovered the impact of circumstances on our behavior. Heredity, environment, wealth, poverty—they all affect the things we do.

We often explain away violent criminal acts with the circumstances surrounding the one who committed the crime. Perhaps a man was brutalized as a child or forced into crime by his poverty. A national magazine recently reported on the discovery that a slight imbalance in one's hormones may incline someone to commit acts of violence.

Circumstances do affect our behavior. But are we not paying an enormous price for this new consciousness of things that *explain* our wrongdoing? Is our society better off with all of these explanations of our behavior? What has happened to our sense of personal responsibility? It is possible that the more we rationalize and excuse our behavior and the behavior of others, the more we will see the breakdown of decency in our society.

Victor Hugo, in his classic work *Les Miserables* told of the fate of Jean Valjean. Jean stole a loaf of bread to feed his starving family. He was held just as responsible for that crime as if he had stolen for pleasure. He was sentenced to five years in prison at hard labor. The experiences of prison life turned him into a hardened criminal. Only when Jean Valjean was befriended by someone who believed he could live a new life did he actually become a new person. Even then society would not forget his one act of theft. Jean lived out his life as a persecuted man.

This was the author's way of saying that the offenders can also be the victims. Jean Valjean would never have stolen the loaf of bread if he had not been driven to it by the cruelties of his age. Victor Hugo was writing to awaken the conscience of his society to the effects of poverty on our behavior. We cannot read his story without understanding some of the factors that drive people to crime.

During the same period when Hugo wrote for the French, Charles Dickens was trying to help the British understand the effects of poverty. Dickens portrayed young waifs whose circumstances turned them to a life of petty thievery. Meanwhile, society showed no understanding of the forces that led these youths to crime. Dickens introduces us to the desperation of their world.

Whose Fault Is It?

Today we have even more sophisticated means for explaining human behavior. Psychology has helped us to understand how forces deep within us can affect our attitudes and actions. An unhappy childhood, uncaring or abusive parents, a domineering father—any of these can have an impact on us. Sociology has shown us how poverty can lead to despair, and despair can lead to crime. It is true that the criminals are often victims themselves.

T. S. Eliot's play *The Family Reunion* portrays a sensitive and sympathetic character who, on a sudden impulse, pushed his wife overboard in a storm. Much could have been said to excuse him. His act was not premeditated; he was not a murderous person. His wife had been terribly selfish and insanely possessive. Heredity was against him; years earlier his father had been on the verge of killing his own wife. This character protested, "It [the deed] was not mine, it was not really I who did it. Nothing that I did has to do with me."

His explanation might be accepted by many today. But what happens to society if we accept explanations that take away our responsibility? More than a decade ago Karl Menninger wrote an important book entitled *Whatever Became of Sin?* He charged that we have gone so far in explaining people's actions that we no longer hold anyone responsible. "Notions of guilt and sin which formerly served as some restraint on aggression," he wrote, "have become eroded by the presumption that the individual has less to do with his actions than we assumed, and hence any sense of personal responsibility (or guilt) is inappropriate." Menninger admitted that there is always some environmental influence on our actions. But he argued that we can never overlook individual responsibility.

An anonymous author has satirized our tendency to shift blame to others:

> At three I had a feeling of
>   Ambivalence toward my brothers,
> And so it follows naturally
>   I poisoned all my lovers.
> But now I'm happy; I have learned
>   The lesson this has taught;
> That everything I do that's wrong
>   Is someone else's fault.

Henry Fairlie argues in *The Seven Deadly Sins Today* that we have come to the end of the road with excusing our own behavior. He says, "I have for a long time thought that the psychological explanation of the waywardness of our behavior and the sociological explanation of the evils of our own societies have come very nearly to a dead end. They have taken us far, but not very far."

The problem is that our explanations seem only to open the door to new wrongs. If poverty excuses lawlessness, we open the door for everyone who has a grievance against society to act out his anger. If everyone who had an unhealthy childhood is considered justified in unleashing his rage on others without any personal accountability, we will see an ever-increasing amount of crime.

On Being Responsible

The fact is that our environment is not the only factor that influences our behavior. Civilization has progressed because people have learned to restrain themselves and to overcome their impulses. Poverty does not always breed crime, nor does discrimination. These conditions may also produce men and women who rise above the very conditions that tempt some people to wrongdoing.

Victor Hugo's Jean Valjean was one of society's victims. After he went to prison for stealing a loaf of bread, he turned to crime until he met someone who believed in him. Later, he would rescue a young girl from the misery of her poverty. Despite the scars of his imprisonment, Jean went on to lead a good life. Victor Hugo was saying that our circumstances do not have to dictate what we shall become. We are responsible for what we make of our lives.

There is a scene early in the Book of Genesis where Cain was bitter because he felt that he had been treated unfairly. The Lord did not accept his offering, and so Cain was angry. But "The LORD said to Cain, 'Why are you angry, and why has your countenance fallen? If you do well, will you not be accepted? And if you do not do well, sin is couching at the door; its desire is for you but you must master it'" (Gen. 4:6–7). This is the warning of the Bible: sin is "couching at the door; its desire is for you, but you must master it." We are not simply the victims of our circumstances. We can—with the right help—master our circumstances.

To avoid responsibility for our actions is a game as old as the human family. Recall the first sin: the tempter enticed the woman to eat the forbidden fruit, and she in turn enticed her husband. When the Lord asked the man if he had eaten the fruit, Adam answered, "The woman whom thou gavest to be with me, she gave me fruit of the tree, and I ate" (Gen. 3:12). When the Lord said to the woman, "What is this that you have done?" she replied, "The serpent beguiled me, and I ate" (v. 13).

The Bible is telling us that wherever there is sin, there will be the attempt to avoid responsibility. Is this not true in each of our lives? We have ingenious ways of shifting the blame to avoid responsibility. We blame "society" for racial injustice, for spoiling our environment, and for the cruelties that go with poverty. And if we can blame these nebulous cultural forces enough, as if we had no part in shaping our social environment, we can escape the blame ourselves.

This is precisely what the Bible will not allow us to do. As much as Adam and Eve tried to escape their individual guilt, they were held responsible for their behavior. They were sent out of Eden. The Bible says that "therefore the LORD God sent him forth from the garden of Eden, to till the ground from which he was taken. He drove out the man; and at the east of the garden of Eden he placed the cherubim, and a flaming sword which turned every way, to guard the way to the tree of life" (Gen. 3:23–24).

This theme—we are responsible for our actions—runs throughout the Bible. "For the wages of sin is death, but the free gift of God is eternal life in Christ Jesus our Lord" (Rom. 6:23). "For we must all appear before the judgment seat of Christ, so that each one may receive good or evil, according to what he has done in the body" (2 Cor. 5:10).

Jesus told a story to illustrate our responsibility for what we do with our lives (Matt. 25:14–30). A master went away on a journey. Before leaving, he distributed his property to his three servants. To one he gave five talents, to another two talents, to another one talent. When he returned, he demanded an accounting by his servants on how they had used the talents. Two of them had doubled their money by making use of what they had been given. But the one who had

received only one talent could only make excuses to his
master. He had done nothing with the money that had been
left in his trust. He was condemned! His master held him
responsible for how he used the resources that had been left
with him.

The Way to Maturity

We need a realistic way of approaching the whole question
of our responsibility. Three considerations, each based
clearly on the Bible, will help us deal with the question of
what God expects of us.

First, since the Bible leaves no doubt that we are sinners,
we should admit this. We are responsible for what we have
done. As much as we may hesitate to talk about sin, we have
sinned against God. We have done things we regret, things
we are ashamed of. And we have failed to do things we should
have done. We did not give to our children the gift of our
time. We failed to live up to our own standards for ourselves.
The Bible indicates that we should be ashamed of ourselves
and recognize our sins.

In. T. S. Eliot's *The Family Reunion*, the family of the
young man who pushed his wife overboard urged him not to
admit what he had done. He could have excused his behavior
by recalling all of the unusual circumstances. But it was in
confessing his deed that he found peace of mind. The Bible
tells us that we are sinners who are responsible for our deeds.
However, we can turn to God and to his people and be forgiven.

Second, the Bible assures us that we do not have to remain
in misery because of our sins. The Fifty-first Psalm was
written by David, apparently after his crime of adultery and
murder. His words are important because they can also be
our words:

> Have mercy on me, O God, according to thy steadfast love;
> according to thy abundant mercy blot out my transgres-
> sions.
> Wash me throughly from my iniquity, and cleanse me from
> my sin!
> For I know my transgressions, and my sin is ever before me.
> Against thee, thee only, have I sinned, and done what is evil in
> thy sight,
> so that thou art justified in thy sentence
> and blameless in thy judgment (Ps. 51:1–4).

David's words indicate that there is One to whom we can turn when we have done wrong. The New Testament is very clear: Jesus Christ has paid the price for our sins, and he can set us free to live a new life.

Third, the Bible describes a new lifestyle that we can adopt. One of God's greatest compliments to us is that he lays down rules for our living. And these rules are strict. Paul wrote:

> . . . walk by the Spirit, and do not gratify the desires of the flesh. . . . Now the works of the flesh are plain: immorality, impurity, licentiousness, idolatry, sorcery, enmity, strife, jeal-ousy, anger, selfishness, dissension . . . and the like. I warn you, as I warned you before, that those who do such things shall not inherit the kingdom of God (Gal. 5:16, 19–21).

God tells us through this text that we have the capacity to overcome these wrongs.

Of course, we cannot overcome sin on our own. God works in our lives to give us the power to overcome our temptations. In Paul's words, "For God is at work in you, both to will and to work for his good pleasure" (Phil. 2:13).

Our lives will be far healthier if we will only accept our personal responsibility. If we will begin to accept this ac-countability, God offers his help to give us new life. Then we can live heroically above the forces that affect our behavior.

6

Heroic Friendship
Building Powerful Relationships

I read recently about an immigrant to America who was quickly impressed by everyone's interest in his welfare. Wherever he turned, people asked, "How are you?" He was not accustomed to this kind of interest. In his country such questions were asked only by relatives or very close friends. Here, casual acquaintances, clerks in the store, or strangers he had just met would ask. And he would answer in full. He told of his sinus headaches and his colds, appreciating this interest in his well-being.

Then the immigrant noticed something else. Those who asked the question did not wait for an answer. "How are you?"—the kind of inquiry your loved ones might make— had become an empty question. Now he was really confused. How would he know when the question was serious?

Most of us know not to take "How are you?" very seriously when it is asked by someone who does not really know us. The phrase has lost its meaning. Other words have had a similar fate. What, for example, is "a friend"? We meet many friendly people. But what does it mean to have real friends? What does it mean to be a friend?

What amazed the immigrant was the instant familiarity he experienced. We seem to make friends so easily. We work in offices surrounded by others. We drink coffee with them. We share little details about our families. Ours may be the most open society in the world. There are places that specialize in giving us the opportunity to meet people: places for singles, places for the newly divorced, places for couples. We can be on a first-name basis with a variety of people in no time.

Friends and Acquaintances

Does the openness in our society provide us with the kind of friendship we really need? Or have we debased a great word? Have we lost the distinction between an acquaintance and a friend? It is easy to find acquaintances. We have business contacts and clients. We go bowling or to ball games with acquaintances whom we may call friends.

When I think of real friendship, I think of a story in the Bible about two men who were more than acquaintances. David and Jonathan were friends, though their friendship was complicated by the fact that Jonathan was the son of King Saul, and King Saul was insanely jealous of David.

David was the most popular man in Israel. Saul was determined to kill him. He would have succeeded if Jonathan had not protected his friend David from the rage of his father. After David's life had been saved, Jonathan said to him, "Go in peace, forasmuch as we have sworn both of us in the name of the LORD, saying, 'The LORD shall be between me and you, and between my descendants and your descendants, for ever'" (1 Sam. 20:42). Their friendship was more than acquaintance, more than having someone with whom to share leisure time. It was a sacred covenant before the Lord.

This element of commitment to one's friends is what is often missing today. Our society raises severe barriers against friendship. Surveys indicate that few men have close friends at all. Married men have even fewer. We have few friends because our busy lifestyle leaves little place for them. We identify ourselves by what we *do* forty hours each week, not by the relationships we have with others. We are taught from our first days in grade school that competition is important. We try to get ahead of our peers. We are more likely to cultivate "contacts" who can be useful than to cultivate friends.

Martin Marty has written that we need only to look around at modern life to see the fate of the friendless. Look closely at the apartment complexes; they may be as dangerous as battlefields. The impersonal high-rise presents enormous barriers to friendliness. People come here, transplanted from the familiar surroundings where they once talked across the backyard fence. The urban-renewal program took away the little house where an old woman and her husband were making payments when he died. Now she is uprooted from lifelong friends, none of whom remembers to call on her in these new surroundings. A social worker comes by every few weeks. She is friendly, but not a friend. When the old woman dies, case #3024 is closed.

It is not only the old and the economically displaced who are friendless. Look at the luxury high-rise apartments that dot the skylines of our big cities. No social worker comes here. The residents can go out to expensive restaurants every night and find company. They work each day surrounded by colleagues, contacts, and acquaintances. On the elevator they speak to people they have greeted for years, but they still do not know each other's names. Many a busy executive returns alone to a posh apartment after a busy day, and there is no one to greet the homecomer. Countless times during the day he or she has heard the friendly words, "Have a nice day," but they were empty words. Something is missing from this type of life.

Some of these people may have chosen deliberately to avoid making friends. When we have friends, we lose part of our freedom. Frederick Buechner tells of sitting down to a dinner with his mother after months of separation. He had looked forward to the occasion, which included not just mother and son, but two old friends who no longer got to see each other very much. Then, just as they were about to sit down to eat, the telephone rang, and it was for Buechner. Before the friend who was calling could say anything, he burst our weeping. Then he explained that his mother and father and a pregnant sister had been in an automobile accident on the West Coast, and it was uncertain whether any of them would live. He was at the airport waiting for a flight to take him to them. Now he asked, "Can you come and wait with me till the plane leaves?"

Buechner knew that the only human thing to do was to go at once. But instead he told his friend that he had to check on some things first. "Can you call back in ten minutes?" he asked.

In the other room was the dinner that was prepared for this special occasion, complete with the best silver and china. When he told his mother that he must leave, she said it was outrageous that a grown man would have to lean on someone else. Besides, there was nothing anyone could do to help. In a moment, the friend called again and said that he had now gotten hold of himself and that he needed no help.

Buechner says the incident reminded him that the only life worth living is not the life shielded from friends. It is the life that is involved in the lives of others—including their heartbreak, their sickness, their pain.

We may purposely avoid the risks of friendship, for friendship is like marriage and having children in that it involves commitment. These steps are costly, because they open us up to inconvenience. To have family or friends is not to be able to call our time our own. A friend may have a problem and we have to get involved. If a friend dies, the pain lasts a long time. If a friend betrays us, we have to live with the disappointment.

So we retreat into our work where no one will ever inconvenience us! There are at least two consequences of living without friends, and they are both bad. First, if we choose to live this way, we will have no one to call when our own pain comes at 2:00 A.M.! Second, a life that is never inconvenienced is sure to be empty. We "come alive" when there are people to care for: people to spend time with, to laugh with, and even to cry with.

Friendship in Christ

I read recently that Christianity has diminished the importance of friendship. The writer observed that the great philosophers before Christ—Plato, Aristotle, and others—devoted lengthy discussions to the importance of having friends. Then he observed that friendship is a word that is seldom mentioned in the Bible.

Yes, Jesus did emphasize another kind of love. He taught us to love everyone, even the unlovely. One of his greatest lessons was his parable of the good Samaritan—a man who was inconvenienced for the sake of a hated foreigner. And Jesus once observed, "For if you love those who love you, what reward have you? Do not even the tax collectors do the same?" (Matt. 5:46). That is, anyone can love a friend, but Jesus taught a higher standard: "Love your enemies and pray for those who persecute you" (v. 44).

But the Bible does emphasize friendships! Jesus had a circle of followers, and he taught them what it meant to be friends. There was a small circle of twelve disciples. There was a smaller circle comprised of Peter, James, and John, and Jesus spent some critical moments when he took them away with him. The Gospel of John even speaks of the disciple "whom Jesus loved," indicating that Jesus had a closest friend (John 13:23).

Then there was a wider circle of friends. The Gospel of John records one busy day in Jesus' life when he was inconvenienced by his friends. He said to his disciples, "Our friend Lazarus has fallen asleep, but I go to awake him out of sleep" (John 11:11). Lazarus had died. Jesus interrupted his work to go and raise Lazarus from the dead.

There is no more powerful statement of the meaning of friendship than when Jesus said to his disciples:

Greater love has no man than this, that a man lay down his life for his friends. You are my friends if you do what I command you. No longer do I call you servants, for the servant does not know what his master is doing; but I have called you friends, for all that I have heard from my Father I have made known to you (John 15:13–15).

Jesus was willing to suffer the ultimate inconvenience for his friends—the inconvenience of dying for them. They were to respond to his love by showing their love for one another.

We do not have to live out our lives with only acquaintances and no friends. It is possible, even in a large city, to have friends who will interrupt their schedules for us, even if it is the middle of the night.

But I especially want to point to the friendship we have in the community of believers—the church. If the Bible does not often speak of friendship, it is because another concept was emphasized. The church is a *family* composed of brothers and sisters in Christ. "Who are my mother and my brothers?" asked Jesus. "Whoever does the will of God is my brother, and sister, and mother" (Mark 3:33, 35). There were people who left home and family for the sake of Christ. They found at his side a completely new family!

Paul's letters commonly end with a list of greetings from the Christians in one city addressed to the Christians in a distant place. He spoke of "our sister Phoebe," of "Apphia our sister," and of "our brother Apollos." He even spoke of a woman in the church at Rome as his "mother" (Rom. 16:13). Those early Christians knew that they belonged to the same family. They greeted each other with a kiss that was normally reserved for the family (Rom. 16:16).

The apostle John's third letter ends with the words, "Peace be with you. The friends greet you. Greet the friends, every one of them" (3 John 15). Those early Christians found friends and family in the church—people they could turn to for help at the most inconvenient times.

The Elements of Commitment

There are three aspects of friendship that make it different from casual acquaintance. Each of these aspects can be found in the church, and they all involve commitment.

First, friends are present when we need them most, and they care for us when we have nothing to give in return. The Bible presents Jesus as our Friend. He has left behind a community of people who love each other. Paul wrote that these friends should "weep with those who weep" (Rom. 12:15b). Christian friends care!

Second, friendship involves the delight of sharing the good fortune of those who are close to us. "Rejoice with those who rejoice," Paul wrote (Rom. 12:15a). Christians celebrate weddings and births and moments of victory together because they care for each other.

Third, friendship involves the pleasure of doing little acts of kindness for each other without expecting something in return. Paul wrote to the Galatians, ". . . do good to all men, and especially to those who are of the household of faith" (Gal. 6:10).

Anyone who takes the risk of belonging to such a community will sometimes have his or her day interrupted by someone else's needs—but will also have the security of knowing that someone will come at two o'clock in the morning if needed! This kind of relationship is well worth the risk. It calls for heroic commitment to one another.

7

Heroic Protector
A God Worthy of Fear

Jonathan Edwards's sermon entitled "Sinners in the Hands of an Angry God" epitomizes the revivalist preachers who once had an important place in American religion. There were vivid accounts of the horrors awaiting those who disobeyed God. Some of the people who heard these sermons were tormented by the ideal of living up to God's standard. Others, when they thought of God, could picture only a vengeful, demanding Being who was always watching his creatures for signs of failure in them.

Today, most people seem to have outgrown this idea of fearing God. The God they know is understanding, warm, accepting, and even gracious. Perhaps we have really discovered something new and exciting about God. But do we also lose something very important when we outgrow the fear of God?

This is not to suggest that we have become less religious than our forefathers. More people are buying religious books in America than ever before. The opinion polls show that religion remains very popular in our country. A visitor from any other nation would be amazed at the place religion holds in our media—radio, television, magazines, and books. Roughly half of our population attends church with some degree of regularity. Millions more tune in to the "electronic" church.

What Will Religion Do for You?

Lest we think this means that Christianity is strong in America, careful observers remind us that these popular aspects of religion are "consumer oriented." That is, the majority of them appeal to our instincts as consumers by demonstrating what religion will do for us. One book tells us that religion can answer our need for self-esteem. Another explains how the principles of religion can give us economic security in hard times. That is, we are told that if only we will follow Christ, we will be free from financial worry. One TV evangelist tells us how Christianity can salvage our marriage and bring happiness to our family. Still another promises that God will give us peace of mind and freedom from anxiety. The theme of the popular religious media is the benefits of religion for us.

There is some truth in these claims. Our faith does make a difference in our family life, our self-esteem, and our sense of fulfillment. Yet this approach is troubling. While it is partially true, it is also a distortion of the Christian faith. This approach places *us*—our wants, our needs—at the center of the world. Religion becomes a commodity to answer our desires, something for us to use to get what we want.

A movie actress was quoted widely as having said, "God is a living doll." The words approach blasphemy. They trivialize God. If we think of God as a "living doll," we lose the awe and the mystery surrounding God's person. Instead of fearing God, we think of him as existing only to give us what we wanted all along.

Popular religion has helped us discover the love and the grace of God, and we may be glad that it has. We have learned that Jesus associated with all kinds of sinners—prostitutes, tax collectors, people who were not "religious." We have learned that Jesus was willing to accept these people despite

what they had done to their lives. What we may have overlooked is that Jesus also demanded that they turn their lives
around. God loves sinners, but he also calls on sinners to
change!

C. S. Lewis, the British writer, once observed that what
many of us want is not a father in heaven, but a grand-
father—an indulgent old man who caters to our wants and
spoils us. This kind of God would never demand anything
from us. He would not hold us accountable for what we do.

The Loving and Demanding God

Today's "consumer's religion," which promises us that all
our wants and needs will be taken care of but makes no
demands of us, is not the faith of the Bible. It may fill church
buildings. It may sell books and involve millions of people
who have never had any religious commitment. But it is a
distortion.

During World War II, a substitute was devised as a coffee
additive because there was a shortage of coffee. As the shortage became more severe, more of the additive was included
in the real product. At some point one had to conclude that
what one was drinking was no longer coffee. This is also true
with our faith. If an essential ingredient is replaced by something else, it ceases to be the faith of the Bible.

The Bible teaches that God is both loving and holy. The
God who graciously saved a helpless group of slaves from
Egypt later stood before them at Mount Sinai with his holy
demands. Do you recall that scene when Moses stood before
God at Sinai? "On the morning of the third day there were
thunders and lightnings, and a thick cloud upon the mountain, and a very loud trumpet blast, so that all the people who
were in the camp trembled" (Exod. 19:16). No one would
come near the mountain for fear of being destroyed. Then
the holy God delivered the commandments that would rule
Israel's life.

In the Bible, men and women trembled before God and his demands. The prophet Isaiah saw a vision of God in the temple and cried out, "Woe is me! For I am lost; for I am a man of unclean lips, and I dwell in the midst of a people of unclean lips; for my eyes have seen the King, the LORD of hosts!" (Isa. 6:5) The psalmist wrote, "Come and see what God has done: he is terrible in his deeds among men" (Ps. 66:5).

The God of the Bible is a loving God, but he is never anyone's "buddy." Paul described God in his letter to the Romans: "Note then the kindness and the severity of God . . ." (Rom. 11:22). We have a difficult time holding together the "kindness and the severity" of God. Some want to speak only of God's loving kindness, and others want to recognize only his stern demands. In the Bible, the two can never be separated. The one who loves us as we are also says, "Go, and do not sin again" (John 8:11).

The Fear That Destroys Fears

It seems to take a crisis of earth-shattering proportions to produce new heroes and villains. World War II certainly produced both. One of the villains was a Norwegian leader named Quisling. While other Norwegians defied the Nazi occupation, Quisling worked for the Nazis. His name became synonymous with betrayal.

One of the heroes among the Norwegians was a leader whose name never became widely known outside of Norway. Eivind Berggrav was a church leader in Oslo. During the Nazi persecution he said, "Have you noticed how full of life the Bible has become, as if written for people in war and during times of occupation?" As Quisling's men took him by car to his prison, Berggrav took out his New Testament and read, "Have no fear of them, nor be troubled, but in your hearts reverence Christ as Lord . . ." (1 Peter 3:14b–15a). This same passage speaks of Christians being ready to defend their faith before hostile listeners "with gentleness and respect" (v. 15b, NIV). Peter insisted that those who reverently fear God can face hostility without being afraid of men.

Another leader in the resistance against the Nazis recalled his interrogation before the local court. He remembered looking around and realizing for the first time that those who were most terrified were not the ones on trial for their convictions. Those who were most fearful were the ones who had sacrificed every conviction to save their own skins.

This is a persistent theme in the Bible. The fear of God liberates us from the fear of others. Those of us who have never known the fear of God are the ones most likely to cave in to the kinds of fears we experience in society.

When Peter wrote to Christians who were an oppressed minority group, he knew they had every reason to be afraid. Their neighbors resented their new ways in Christ. Sometimes the Christians were asked to defend their beliefs, which seemed very strange to others. It was in that situation that Peter said, ". . . Have no fear of them, nor be troubled, but in your hearts reverence Christ as Lord. Always be prepared to make a defense to any one who calls you to account for the hope that is in you, yet do it with gentleness and reverence" (1 Peter 3:14b–15). It was the fear of God that allowed them to stand confidently before people who despised their faith and speak their convictions without fear.

When Peter wrote those words, he was recalling some advice given eight centuries earlier by Isaiah. Israel was being threatened by the conquering Assyrians. Rumors were flying about the terror of the Assyrians. Isaiah said to his people that the Lord had told him: "Do not call conspiracy all that this people call conspiracy, and do not fear what they fear, nor be in dread. But the LORD of hosts, him you shall regard as holy: let him be your fear, and let him be your dread" (Isa. 8:12–13). The only thing that could free the people from panic before the Assyrians was their fear of God.

Is it not amazing that those very words, spoken in the eighth century B.C. when the Assyrians were coming, were appropriate at the end of the first century A.D. when Chris-

tians were facing hostile neighbors? Even more amazing is
that those same words provided strength for people who
were taken to jail by the Nazis in the twentieth century.
Those who fear God are least likely to be intimidated in a
moment of crisis.

The heroes of the Bible were people of extraordinary courage. In the eleventh chapter of Hebrews, we are given an
entire catalog of courageous men and women who acted on
their convictions about God. We are told that Moses' parents
"were not afraid of the king's edict" (v. 23). Pharaoh had
ordered that all of the small male children be killed. But
Moses' mother hid him and saved his life.

Then we are told of the difficult decision Moses made
when he became a grown man: "By faith he left Egypt, not
being afraid of the anger of the king; for he endured as seeing
him who is invisible" (Heb. 11:27). Others could see only the
terrors of the moment—the anger of the king, the hostility
of their neighbors. But those who feared God could endure.
They could see something that others could not see.

Near the end of the letter to the Hebrews, there is a beautiful paragraph where the author recalled the terrors of
Mount Sinai—the lightning, the thunder, the fire that struck
terror in the hearts of Moses and the Israelites. Then he
added, "For you have not come to what may be touched, a
blazing fire, and darkness, and gloom, and a tempest. . . .
Indeed, so terrifying was the sight that Moses said, 'I tremble
with fear.' But you have come to Mount Zion and to the city
of the living God, the heavenly Jerusalem, and to innumer-
able angels in festal gathering" (Heb. 12:18–22). The writer
was saying that what Christians face is far more awesome
than the terrors of Mount Sinai! We stand before God himself—"For our God is a consuming fire" (v. 29).

Sometimes our worship seems so very ordinary. We go
through the same routines week after week. Our life as
Christians may seem so commonplace that we take all of it
for granted. The Bible keeps calling us back to a realization of
the One we worship: the consuming fire, the living God, our

heroic protector! We dare not offer him anything but our best.

Some of us may want to have the love of God without the fear of God. And others may understand the wrath of God but fail to understand his love. But the God of the Bible is both "a consuming fire" and he is "love." Once we learn to stand before him in awe, we will have the courage not to be intimidated by a culture that thinks our faith and our worship are absurd.

8

Heroic Search
Finding God's Place in Our Lives

For at least two hundred years, informed people have been predicting that "religion" would disappear. And they seem to have a lot of evidence. Imagine those medieval towns where religion was present everywhere and controlled everyone's life. Or those Puritan villages where the influence of the church was so deep that the preachers made the laws.

The sociologists have a point when they say that religion has lost its influence over our culture. The civil laws no longer reflect the wishes of the churches. Fully half of our population has almost no contact with organized religion. The churches and synagogues remain as places for significant moments in our lives—birth, marriage, death—but they have little daily importance for many of us.

We will likely never return to the days of the Puritans, when the impact of organized religion was felt everywhere in society. But it appears equally certain that the time has not come to write the epitaph on religion! The reason is simple: whether we go to church or not, whether we believe the religion of our parents or not, we are deeply religious. Religion is a hunger that is as deeply rooted in us as the hunger and thirst for food and drink.

The Effort to Eradicate Religion

Some unusual efforts have been made in recent years to pretend that religion has no place in our lives. We are not supposed to talk about religion in the public schools. Libertarians say that school is the place where we talk about things that are real! So we limit our conversation to the test tube or the mathematical formula or the set of statistics. We memorize dates and places for the history exam and read the literary works of the past to become "educated." But religion is left out.

Someone studied a number of history textbooks recently and made a startling discovery. In many of them religion had been so erased from the story that the events did not make sense. Imagine telling about Joan of Arc without referring to religion! Or trying to teach American history without referring to religion! The pilgrims, Thanksgiving, the abolitionists, the civils-rights struggle—one cannot tell these stories without noting the religious drive that led people to sacrifice for a cause. The very thing that ignited many American heroes has been omitted from our history books.

Heroes never arise where the only real thing in the world is what one can analyze in a test tube. No one ever died for a mathematical equation.

Regular television programming likewise presents a world where religion does not exist. Almost no one among the families on television goes to church. No one seems to ask religious or ethical questions. Of all the documentaries on AIDS, the problem seems to be treated as a technological and scientific issue, never as a religious and ethical one.

If we ask why religion has disappeared from the secular media, the answer may be that the media reflect life. Religion does not appear in our sit-coms and our dramas because it no longer exists where we are living.

Organized religion does appear to be on the decline. But this does not mean that we are no longer religious. There is a world of difference between being religious and being involved in organized religion. Is there any person who does not ask religious questions? Even people who go from one entertainment to another display an emptiness, a boredom, a restless search for something that is missing from their lives. This emptiness is a religious hunger for something more out of life, something one cannot find in moving from one chic nightclub to another.

The seventeenth-century French philosopher Pascal wrote, "I have discovered that all human evil comes from this: man's being unable to sit still in a room." Things have not changed much, have they? We are still restless, busy. Is it because we are trying to ignore the hunger for meaning in our lives?

Our Craving for Purpose

Life without the religious dimension becomes a dull routine. We get married; a child is born (or not born); we take a job and go to work day after day. Our routine is the same, week after week. The weeks and months slip into years. Then one day we ask what we are actually doing with our lives. Is there any design behind the routine days and nights? What are we becoming? What do we make of ourselves?

We have a need to tie together all of the days and nights into one purpose, and that is religious hunger. Religion, to paraphrase Robert Frost, begins with "a lump in the throat."

When the pain we feel finally leads us to a doctor for an examination, we anxiously wait for the medical report. We have not thought about praying for a long time. We are not sure what we believe about prayer. But this moment of anxiety leads us to pray, even if we do not understand how prayer works or what God is like.

The stories about Jesus in the Bible are filled with episodes of people who came crying to him because their world had been shattered by pain. Until such a moment comes in our own lives, we may think that the real world is the one we can get our hands on—the promotion, the bigger house and

car. Then we utter the cry for help that our possessions cannot answer. And the religious quest begins.

If we look carefully, we will see that we are not a people
without "religious" fervor. We are all busy choosing our ultimate commitments. It may be the climb up the corporate
ladder that makes us sacrifice family and relationships. Viktor Frankl has an interesting essay in which he says that the
religion of the twentieth century is sports. What else can
draw out the commitment and passion of so many people?

Nutritionists remind us that we Americans have a bad
habit of satisfying our hunger with junk food. For the moment, the junk food takes away our hunger. But lasting good
health depends on satisfying our appetite with good nutrition. It is the same way with our religious hunger. We are all
hungry, and we must choose between junk food and real
nutrition.

Joseph: A Case Study

One of the most delightful Broadway plays in recent years
was *Joseph and the Amazing Technicolor Dreamcoat.* The
music and the lyrics were moving. Even before this play was
staged, no Bible story could better capture our imagination.
The story is powerful because it has a genuine hero, a be-
lievable character whose life had much in common with our
own.

When we first begin reading the story of Joseph, he seems
to be one of those tragic figures who will make the inevitable
mistakes that will bring about his own destruction. Joseph
grew up as a favorite among his father's twelve sons. We
could easily predict what is sure to happen to the favorite
child.

First, his father added to the child's woes by making
him—and only him—that special coat of many colors.
Then, as if Joseph could not help himself, he "rubbed it in"
by reminding his brothers constantly of his special place. He

told them his dreams about the days when they would bow down before him.

Little by little, the relationship was so poisoned that finally, in the words of the play, the brothers said, "This dreamer has got to go." They arranged to sell him into slavery. They told their grieving father that the boy had been killed by a wild animal. If the story had ended here, we might have concluded that Joseph was a tragic figure, doomed by his father's favoritism and his own ego.

Even if we pick up the story a little later, we still conclude that Joseph was dealt a bad hand in life. He became a slave in Egypt. Then he rose to a position of power in Potiphar's house. When he refused the advances of Potiphar's wife, he lost his favorite position and wound up in jail.

Of course, this story did not end there. The time came when Pharaoh needed Joseph. This dreamer understood Pharaoh's mysterious dreams. He helped plan for Egypt's lean years by suggesting a policy of saving the food supplies from the good years. Once again Joseph was restored to a position of power. He became Pharaoh's personal planner and adviser.

Finally the threads all came together when Joseph's brothers came to Egypt to replenish their food supplies in a time of famine. Joseph had the power of life and death over them, the opportunity for revenge. The beauty of the story is that Joseph used the moment not for revenge but for reconciliation. The brother who had been sold into slavery became the one who saved those who had plotted against him. Jacob, now an old man, could see the son for whom he had grieved and could later die in peace. The Book of Genesis has a happy ending!

Joseph must have wondered during the years whether anything made sense in life. We read his story today because, even when he did not see how the threads would come together, he lived with a strong belief in the providence of God. This conviction gave him the courage to refuse Potiphar's

wife. Joseph was not living for the moment but for the long
view of things. His faith gave him the courage to endure
months and years in prison. Even if he could not see the
outcome, he knew that life would make sense some day.

A favorite paragraph in the Bible for many is that moment
when his brothers stood before him in fear, wondering how
Joseph would get his revenge. Instead of seeking revenge,
Joseph said, "As for you, you meant evil against me; but God
meant it for good, to bring it about that many people should
be kept alive, as they are today. So do not fear; I will provide
for you and your little ones" (Gen. 50:20–21a).

We are all religious. We all want to know if life makes any
sense. With Joseph, we wonder if any plot is being played out
in our lives. We see reports on the nightly news of tragedies
that do not make sense. Such movies as *Platoon* remind us of
the little people who are caught up in the tragedy of wars
they did not make. Their lives are at stake in a world they
cannot control.

Search for the Plot

We all share the same questions. Is there a purpose in our
lives? Do these little episodes ever add up to one single plot?
Do the loose threads—the disappointments, the heartbreak,
the illness—ever come together? We ask the questions, but
where do we turn for answers?

Many people turn to religious "junk food." One person
makes the ultimate goal of his or her life to acquire things.
Another seeks power. Another, pleasure. These pursuits
might make suitable hobbies, but they function poorly as
religion! They do not satisfy the deep hunger we have for
meaning in life.

The ancient prophet Isaiah saw people dabbling in re-
ligions that did not satisfy. He wrote,

Ho, every one who thirsts, come to the waters;
  and he who has no money, come, buy and eat!
Come, buy wine and milk without money and without price.
Why do you spend your money for that which is not bread,
  and your labor for that which does not satisfy?
Hearken diligently to me, and eat what is good,
  and delight yourselves in fatness.
Incline your ear, and come to me;
  hear, that your soul may live;
  and I will make with you an everlasting covenant. . . (Isa.
  55:1–3).

Jesus knew that we have this hunger of the soul. He said, "Blessed are those who hunger and thirst for righteousness, for they shall be satisfied" (Matt. 5:6). Our faith in God and in his son Jesus Christ can satisfy this deep hunger.

One of the greatest crises faced in this century is the emptiness of having no goal or purpose in life. This does not have to be so, if we will but recognize the plot that is playing in our lives. Understanding God's place in our lives can fulfill our "heroic search" for meaning.

PART 2

Ken Durham

9

Heroic Expectation
Shaping a Realistic Life View

In a file folder marked "Heroes," I collect newspaper and magazine accounts of heroic actions and lives. For instance, I have a *New York Times* clipping about an elderly black woman in Harlem called Mother Hale, who provides foster care for the babies of drug addicts and now plans to do the same for infants born with AIDS. There's a *Time* magazine story about a dramatic event you may remember, that airline crash into the Potomac River in Washington a few winters ago, where an unidentified man passed the helicopter lifeline to five other people so they might be airlifted to safety, only to lose his own life.

I also keep a clipping from my hometown paper, about a woman named Nancy Nickerson, who for years organized and taught classes for disabled persons all over our area. She lost the use of her hands to polio, so she did all this with her feet. She typed with her feet, drove a car with her feet, served people with her feet.

When I begin to get a little disillusioned or cynical about my fellow man and woman, sometimes I pull out this file and fix my mind on some authentic heroes. More often, I pull out my New Testament and take a long, hard look at Jesus of Nazareth and fix my gaze on the Hero of heroes.

A recent *New York Times* article asked, "Where Have All the Heroes Gone?" suggesting that "Americans seem at a loss for a clear understanding of the term." Have we really lost the eye for a hero when we see one? Perhaps we have come to confuse the hero with the celebrity, the lifestyle of the good and heroic with "Lifestyles of the Rich and Famous."

In Harold Kushner's popular book *When All You've Ever Wanted Isn't Enough*, he discusses the deep discontentment and boredom we see in the eyes of so many around us. He writes:

> Our souls are not hungry for fame, comfort, wealth, or power. Those rewards create almost as many problems as they solve. Our souls are hungry for meaning, for the sense that we have figured out how to live so that our lives matter, so that the world will be at least a little bit different for our having passed through it.

God meant our lives to have meaning and focus and usefulness and joy. That's what "heroic living" is—not necessarily life that is always successful or applauded or even happy all the time—but life that makes a difference.

A Book for the Discontented

If you are among the chronically disillusioned, or even the occasionally discontented, I want to introduce you to a fascinating book in the Bible. Way back in the Old Testament, among pages that seldom get turned, is a book that opens with this melancholy cry: "Meaningless! Meaningless! Everything is meaningless!" (NIV). Doesn't sound much like Scripture, does it? But it is. This is the cry of the writer of Ecclesiastes.

The writer, identified as "the Teacher" in the New International Version and thought by many to be King Solomon, expresses disillusionment with just about everything. His favorite word is "meaningless" (or "vanity" in other versions). Among his complaints are these:

1. *Life's just not fair.* "There is something else meaningless that occurs on earth: righteous men who get what the wicked deserve, and wicked men who get what the righteous deserve" (8:14, NIV).

2. *Knowledge and education are no magic wand.* "I devoted myself to study and to explore by wisdom all that is done under heaven. . . . I have seen all the things that are done under the sun; all of them are meaningless, a chasing after the wind" (1:13–14, NIV).

3. *The "good life" is just not what it's cracked up to be.* "I thought in my heart, 'Come now, I will test you with pleasure to find out what is good.' But that also proved to be meaningless. 'Laughter,' I said, 'is foolish. And what does pleasure accomplish?' . . . I denied myself nothing my eyes desired; I refused my heart no pleasure. . . . everything was meaningless, a chasing after the wind . . ." (2:1–2, 10–11, NIV).

4. *I just don't understand how God works sometimes.* "I have seen another evil under the sun, and it weighs heavily on men: God gives a man wealth, possessions and honor, so that he lacks nothing his heart desires, but God does not enable him to enjoy them, and a stranger enjoys them instead. This is meaningless . . ." (6:1–2, NIV).

Have you ever felt those frustrations? Are you surprised to hear a biblical writer expressing them so honestly and bluntly? One of the wonderfully genuine qualities of Scripture is the way it gives such candid expression to our greatest doubts and struggles, both emotional and philosophical. It is hard to come up with a complaint against God that is not already contained in God's Word!

You Can't Always Get What You Want

The Big Chill was a movie about the disappointments of adulthood. It opens as a group of college friends are reunited,

many years after graduation, at the funeral of a friend who
has committed suicide. At the close of the funeral, one of the
women walks to the front of the church and begins to play on
the organ "You Can't Always Get What You Want," a song
popularized by the Rolling Stones.

Well, you *can't* always get what you want. And life does
not often seem fair. "The Teacher" pondered this:

> The race is not always to the swift or the battle to the strong,
> nor does food come to the wise or wealth to the brilliant or
> favor to the learned; but time and chance happen to them all
> (9:11, NIV).

The words of Ecclesiastes have a very modern ring to
them. They remind me of Kurt Vonnegut's sadly funny book,
Slaughterhouse Five, in which the narrator, Billy Pilgrim,
encounters one human tragedy after another, always with
the same pessimistic words: "So it goes."

But is that the message God wants us to hear from Ecclesiastes? No, there is more to the teacher's message than to
bring us to the fatalistic acceptance, "That's just the way the
cookie crumbles." Amidst the darkness of this writer's disillusionment, light begins to break forth. And hope. And
faith. If we stick with him, he will offer some pretty sage
advice on the way to his grand "end of the matter" (11:13).

Advice for the Disillusioned

Here are some examples of what we might call "The
Teacher's Honest Advice for the Chronically Disillusioned":

1. *See life in its totality.* Perhaps the single most familiar
passage in Ecclesiastes is the one that reminds us of life's
changeability:

> There is a time for everything, and a season for every activity
> under heaven: a time to be born and a time to die, a time to
> plant and a time to uproot, a time to kill and a time to heal, a

time to tear down and a time to build, a time to weep and a
time to laugh. . . (3:1–4, NIV).

Life is made up of all of these, the bitter and the sweet, the
ugly and the beautiful, the peaks and the valleys. Our experience tells us that is true. That is why a marriage vow must be
a promise made to endure "in sickness and in health, for
richer or for poorer, for better or for worse."

None of us will escape the tremendous variety of experiences that make up life in God's reality. Why God made life
thus I cannot say, but this much I know: when he sent his
Son to live among us, he played by his own rules. For Jesus
there was birth and death, weeping and laughing, the whole
range of the total human experience. Our Hero of heroes
lived through all our seasons.

2. *Enjoy your life now, as you have the opportunity.* As I
read through Ecclesiastes, I get a picture of the writer at
times pausing as he simmers down and stops shaking his fist
at God for a moment, because he realizes: Why, every good
thing I have—my food, my work, my possessions, my life—
"this is the gift of God" (5:19). And in this spirit he counsels:

> Go, eat your food with gladness, and drink your wine with a
> joyful heart, for it is now that God favors what you do. Always
> be clothed in white, and always anoint your head with oil.
> Enjoy life with your wife, whom you love. . . (9:7–9, NIV).

This teacher is a frank realist. He writes of days of light
and days of darkness (11:7–8) and the inevitable day when
"man goes to his eternal home and the mourners go about
the streets" (12:5). We are all terminal, he says, every last one
of us.

So, accepting that reality, let us make the most of our
times of good health and favor. Relish a good meal. Spruce
up; it will make you feel better. (Depressed people often
dress depressed, don't they?) And if you are married, rejoice
in that relationship. Love that spouse of yours. Shower the
people you love with love.

3. *Cast your bread on the waters.* As long as our disillusioned teacher pursued pleasure, and hoarded "good life" experiences, he found himself empty, unsatisfied, meaningless. But he learned that when we begin generously to share our bounty with others, we will reap a return of fullness, satisfaction, and meaning.

Cast your bread upon the waters, for you will find it after many days (11:1).

You have no doubt seen that grand old Christmastime movie, *It's a Wonderful Life,* where the character played by Jimmy Stewart finds out—at a point of suicidal despair—just what a rich man he is, because he has invested his life in people.

As I understand the heroic lifestyle, this is a fundamental principle. Invest in people. Like Mother Hale. And Nancy Nickerson. And the man in the Potomac, who gave his life for five others. And Jesus, who gave his life for every man and woman who have ever walked the face of this frustrating, wonderful planet.

4. *Worship the only One who gives meaning to life, the Lord God.* The writer of Ecclesiastes has complained and pouted, examined this and that possible pathway to happiness, and now is finally ready to give us his final verdict. Here it is:

Now all has been heard; here is the conclusion of the matter: Fear God and keep his commandments, for this is the whole duty of man (12:13, NIV).

This teacher has led us on an exploration of some deep waters, and has done it like my wife explores a box of chocolates. Cathy's very particular with chocolates. She takes a bite of one. No. And puts it back. She tries another. No. Another. No, no, no. Finally, yes, that's it!

Our teacher looks at all the possible sources of happiness and meaningfulness. Success? Meaningless. Pleasure? Vanity. Education? No. Possessions? No. God? *Yes!*

Fear God and keep his commandments. Of him we can be sure. He will lead us in the paths to heroic living. In him we find the reason to face every season of life with courage, to relish every blessing with joy, to invest ourselves in people. Let us worship and obey him.

This wise writer has served us well. He has led us in search of contentment and meaning. He has bluntly verbalized some of our deepest frustrations and toughest questions. And he has challenged us to find our fulfillment in enjoying life, serving people, and worshiping God.

In the next chapters let us return to the New Testament for a long, hard look at the lifestyle of the Hero of heroes.

10

Heroic Power
Rediscovering the Power of Servanthood

On a Sunday in May of 1927, the bold front-page headline of *The New York Times* announced: "Lindbergh Does It! To Paris in 33½ Hours; Flies 1000 Miles Through Snow and Sleet; Cheering French Carry Him Off the Field." When Captain Charles A. Lindbergh flew "The Spirit of St. Louis" from New York to Paris in 1927, he became a bona-fide American hero, a true pioneer—he had accomplished something that had never been done before, a nonstop transatlantic flight.

Today, dozens of jumbo jets leave Kennedy Airport daily, bound for Paris. But Lindbergh was the first. He led the way into a new era. And, after him, aviation was never the same again.

Jesus is described in the New Testament Book of Hebrews as mankind's "pioneer" (2:10; 12:2). Using the language of the Jewish temple, the writer pictures him as the heroic High Priest who blazes for us "a new and living way" into the once-forbidden Holy of Holies, where we may draw near to God himself (10:19–22). But this Pioneer is more than just a trailblazer from yesterday's headlines. He is the ever-present Hero who understands the struggle we pilgrims experience as we make our way along the trail today: "For because he himself has suffered and been tempted, he is able to help those who are tempted" (2:18).

A Hero's Power

When we think of a genuine hero, we think of *power*—the means or ability to get things done, to move people to action. Abraham Heschel wrote, "History is first of all what man does with power."

How to get and use power for one's personal advantage is a popular current topic. In his best-seller, *Unlimited Power,* Anthony Robbins calls power "the commodity of kings" and "the ability to direct your own personal kingdom." Power is volatile, fascinating, seductive, thrilling. Power succeeds and power achieves. But power also consumes and corrupts.

Jesus was a powerful man, possessor of the magnificent power of God Almighty. When he unleashed his power, withered legs were rebuilt, rotten skin was made as soft and pink as a baby's bottom, and violent winds and waves were spoken into silent submission. He could make wine out of tapwater, and a picnic for thousands out of a sack lunch for one. He took a modest band of twelve men, trained them in a small, underdeveloped, occupied nation, and forged a nucleus of believers who would change history. Never has so much power lived in one man.

But what—and this is a crucial question—what was Jesus' *strategy* of power? What was his agenda? What his master power-plan? The biblical answer, I believe, is that his power strategy was servanthood. Sum up his power in one word and you would have to call it "servant power."

Jesus was, and is, a king like no other, the King of what someone has called an "Upside-Down Kingdom." Speaking of himself, Jesus said, "For the Son of man also came not to be served but to serve, and to give his life as a ransom for many" (Mark 10:45). ". . . I am among you as one who serves" (Luke 22:27b). Jesus took the world's power-pyramid and turned it upside down.

A Kingdom of Servants

Jesus came to be the Chief Servant, overseeing a kingdom of servants. If the idea of being a citizen in a servant kingdom strikes you as not altogether attractive, you are not alone. As a minister, I struggle with it. The New Testament word for "minister" is *diakonos*—it means "servant; one who waits on tables." In other words, if you walked into an eating establishment in the first century and sat down at a table littered with dirty plates and greasy food scraps, you might yell, "Hey, send a minister over here to clean up this mess!" Long before it meant clergyman or preacher, "minister" meant (and I assume still means) "servant."

Have you ever noticed how Jesus' anger burned hottest when he encountered religious people—leaders in particular—who had forgotten how to be servants? In Matthew 23, he severely chastised those Jewish leaders who seemed to be in the kingdom business just for the personal glory, for the titles and the places of honor. It is awfully hard to serve from the top of a high-altitude pedestal. As Jesus evaluates today's religious leaders and how they use their power, are his standards any different? I doubt that they are.

In the upside-down kingdom of Jesus Christ, the power is that of God, and the strategy is that of servanthood. Power is a gift to be used in ministering to people, not a device to be used in manipulating and controlling them. The symbols of this king's sovereignty are not the crown jewels but a crown of thorns; not a scepter but a dirty towel; not a throne but a cross.

In his kingdom, there is no caste system—neither Jew nor Gentile; black nor white; slave nor free; lower, middle, or upper class; male nor female—no second-class citizens. But

all are servants, and "all are one in Christ Jesus," the King
(Gal. 3:28).

Unleashing Servant Power

A wise preacher was once asked, "How many points
should a sermon have?" And his answer was, "At least one."
Have you caught the one point of this chapter? If you have
missed it, here it is again: the heroes, the power people in
Jesus' kingdom are all *servants*. But for most of us, unleashing the power of servanthood in our lives means overcoming
our desire always to be Number One, to compete with James
and John for the best seats in the kingdom (Mark 10:35–45).
A servant must learn from God to:

1. *Quit worrying about getting enough respect.* Rodney
Dangerfield has built a successful career around one line: "I
don't get no respect!" Did you ever notice that Jesus never
made that complaint? He could easily have said, "Wait a
minute, don't you know who I am? You don't treat the Son of
God that way!" But he never did. When God was not getting
proper respect, or when others were not being properly loved
and respected, *then* Jesus got angry!

Think how many acts of service we have failed to perform
because a devilish little voice whispered in our ear, "Hey,
that's beneath you! You're too dignified for that, too educated, too sophisticated, too good for that menial kind of
service." Remember: Jesus, the most powerful man who
ever lived, washed the feet of his friends. We must not let our
"respectability" get in the way of servanthood; the King
never did.

2. *Let others win sometimes.* Can you give up "the thrill
of victory" once in a while? I live on a busy street in Stam-
ford, Connecticut, right where two lanes merge into one.
And all day long it's driver-versus-driver in heated competition for that coveted lead position going into the one lane—
honking horns, screeching tires, and shouted words I really
don't care to have my kids learn.

This is deeply engrained in us, isn't it? To compete, to win, to be Number One. But we will never take those initiatives of servanthood if we approach life as one big Super Bowl. Let's hear the words of Paul the apostle:

Do nothing out of selfish ambition or vain conceit, but in humility consider others better than yourselves. Each of you should look not only to your own interests, but also to the interests of others. Your attitude should be the same as that of Christ Jesus (Phil. 2:3–5, NIV).

Let the other guy get the credit sometimes. Learn to rejoice in someone else's victory besides your own. Practice your servanthood out of the limelight, where no one can see it but God.

3. *Get your hands dirty.* While there is no inherent virtue in dirt, getting dirty on behalf of others can be beautiful. Again, think of Jesus kneeling down on the night before his death and washing twelve pairs of smelly, dirty feet, including the feet of the very man who would turn him in. In this upside-down kingdom, the One whose sandals we are not worthy to unloose shows us the beauty of selfless servanthood as he loosens the sandals of his own betrayer.

Here's a simple servanthood exercise (and test): The next time you are in a public washroom and you see a paper towel on the floor by the trash can, pick it up. "But I didn't put it there!" you say. (That's exactly what my kids would say.) Wait till nobody is looking, so no one but you and the Lord will know, and pick it up—a simple, menial, unapplauded act of service to others. You may want to wash your hands afterwards, but I guarantee you will feel good for it.

4. *Make a sacrifice.* The oldest form of worship—as far back as Cain and Abel—is the offering of a sacrifice to God. Our Hebrew forefathers of faith gave Yahweh the best lamb for sacrifice—the prize, the beauty, the pride and joy. Only the best for Yahweh.

I am not sure that the principle of sacrifice is as well understood today as it was in ancient Israel. A local benevolent agency puts out a call for clothing for the poor. So we go to our closets: "Let's see. Here's a shirt with an ink stain on the pocket; I'll give them that. And these pants with a seat worn so thin I can see right through them; yeah, I'll give them up. And here's my old plaid sports coat—man, I wouldn't be caught dead in that!" And thus we make our sacrificial offering.

"Therefore, I urge you, brothers, in view of God's mercy, to offer yourselves as living sacrifices, holy and pleasing to God—which is your spiritual worship" (Rom. 12:1, NIV). God asks a lot of us, doesn't he? Not just our best lamb or our best sports coat, but our very selves and all that is best and heroic about us—our energies, our skills, our dreams, our love. And when we place them willingly on his altar, he takes them and fashions from them heroic lives—lives with the greatest power of them all, servant power.

I cannot heal with a touch of my hand, or feed five thousand with a sack lunch, but I can wash a dirty foot, dry a lonely tear, give a cup of cold water in his name. And when I do, in that moment of servanthood, when nobody is looking but God, it is then that I most resemble his Son, the upside-down King.

11

Heroic Communication
Speaking the Truth in Love

This is the Communication Age, no doubt about it. John Naisbitt opens his popular book *Megatrends* with a chapter on our society's explosive "megashift" from an industrial to an *information* society. The communication technology available for the sharing of information is almost magical. When President Lincoln was shot, Naisbitt says, it was five days before London heard the news. When President Reagan was shot, a journalist working within a block of the shooting heard about it quickly—by telephone from his editor in London, who had just seen film of the assassination attempt on British television.

But we forget, even in the Communication Age, just how powerful words are. Cathy and I took our kids to the Bronx Zoo a while back on one of those hot summer days when thousands of other parents had the same idea. Tempers tend to run a bit short in circumstances like that, but you should have heard what I heard parents saying to their kids!

"Okay, go ahead, get lost, just see if I care!"

"What is wrong with you? Why can't you be like that nice little boy over there?"

Material in this chapter was adapted from my book, *Speaking from the Heart* © 1986, Sweet Publishing Co., Ft. Worth, TX.

"You make me sick! I'm ashamed of you! I ought to walk off and leave you here!"

I know our kids can sometimes bring out the worst in us, but are we listening to our words? Did you ever hear a parent refer to his or her child as "our mistake"? No one should have to grow up thinking of himself or herself as a mistake! But then, what parents say to their children is nothing compared to what some parents say to each other.

The Potency of the Spoken Word

"Just words" you say? Just the passage of air over vibrating vocal cords? Let's not kid ourselves. Words are incredibly potent. And we've known that for a long time. The ancient Proverbs of Israel recognized this fact three thousand years ago:

"The tongue has the power of life and death . . ." (18:21, NIV).

"A soft answer turns away wrath, but a harsh word stirs up anger" (15:1).

"Reckless words pierce like a sword, but the tongue of the wise brings healing" (12:18, NIV).

"The tongue that brings healing is a tree of life, but a deceitful tongue crushes the spirit" (15:4, NIV).

If you are one of those folks who say, "Oh, my words don't make any difference," I beg you to reconsider. For the Bible says otherwise. Why, what you can do for another person in "twenty-five words or less" is astounding: "Good job." "That's beautiful." "I'm sorry." "Please forgive me." "I love you." Words do not have to be eloquent or multi-syllabic to be heart-healing and life-changing. Words are powerful.

What is one of the first things your doctor says when you go in for a check-up? Isn't it "let me see your tongue"? Let's engage in a little personal checkup and do it by looking at our tongues.

Again we begin by fixing our eyes on our life's Hero—Jesus—a man who respected the power of words, who used them simply and masterfully. It was said of him, even by his enemies, "No man ever spoke like this man!" (John 7:46). There was something wonderfully uncommon about the way he spoke to people—not just to the multitudes, but one-to-one. And there was something absolutely unprecedented about the way he spoke *of* God and *to* God. What was it?

In Ephesians 4:15, Paul the apostle gives us a good clue, as he offers this high communication standard for the heroic Christian lifestyle: ". . . speaking the truth in love, we will in all things grow up into him who is the Head, that is, Christ" (NIV).

Speaking the truth in love. That simple phrase houses what may be the two noblest qualities of communication, what John Powell was describing when he wrote, "The genius of communication is the ability to be both totally honest and totally kind at the same time" *(The Secret of Staying in Love).* Let's examine those qualities individually.

Speaking the Truth: Honesty

One study found that some people tell as many as fifty lies a day! What are some of our favorite un-truths, or attempts at "dis-information"? How about these:

"I'll get right on it."
"The check's in the mail."
"I was only kidding."
"No, you didn't wake me up" (my personal favorite).

I think we have all grown more than a little skeptical about who's telling us the truth these days. The government? What are they *not* telling us? Advertisers? Are their claims and images really true ones? And let's be honest, how about us people on the religious television programs? Can we be trusted? What's our true agenda? These are legitimate questions, because honesty is essential to healthy living—healthy communication, healthy relationships, healthy decision making, healthy faith.

Jesus knew of our need to hear the truth—about God, about life, about ourselves. A characteristic phrase of his was "Verily, verily," which can also be translated as "I tell you the truth." Honesty was so much a part of his character and mission that he even made this astounding claim: "I *am* the truth" (John 14:6). Jesus, our Hero, was truth with skin, bones, and muscle.

Truth is to human beings as a greenhouse is to beautiful flowers—the best environment for growth and health. A lie frustrates God's purposes for us. Human relationships were not designed to work correctly with deceit and falseness, any more than an automobile was meant to run on tapwater. God created us to "walk in the light, as he is in the light" (1 John 1:7). Only in the light, in an environment of truth, will we grow and flourish and blossom.

The Truth in Love: Kindness

Psycho-linguists are talking today about the dangerously high levels of "verbal violence" in our society—on the TV screen, around the playgrounds, in our bedrooms—language that is overly aggressive, mean-spirited, and punitive.

Verbal violence, the ancient proverbs say, pierces the soul and crushes the spirit. It quenches our joy, brutalizes our self-image, and forms calluses on our heart. But a kind word heals the heart. It lifts the spirit, bolsters self-esteem, reawakens joy.

Garrison Keillor on "Prairie Home Companion" tells about a couple in his fictitious hometown of Lake Wobegon, named Florian and Myrtle Krebsbach. The Krebsbachs are so predictable that every Friday night of their married life, Myrtle has served the same meal: breaded fish fillets. But every Friday, Florian takes that first bite, savors it, and says, "Ah, that's the best you ever did." And he finds something different to compliment, something he hadn't noticed about her breaded fish fillets over the past forty-seven years, which comes to almost twenty-five hundred servings of breaded fish fillets. That's a kind word, and we all need it, everyone.

Jesus knew that we can hear the truth best when it is communicated with an ample amount of kindness and love. When truth wears combat boots, look out! We can state facts that are absolutely irrefutable, but if we speak them harshly or self-righteously, we will do neither ourselves nor the other person much good at all. Put another way: "If I speak in the tongues of men and of angels, but have not love, I am a noisy gong or a clanging cymbal" (1 Cor. 13:1).

One Day in Jerusalem

Go back with me to one of the many days when Jesus spoke the truth in love. Put yourself in the place of a person whose encounter with Jesus is recorded in John 8:1–11:

You are a Jewish woman, and you live in Jerusalem, in the first century A.D. Your life has been pretty much a disappointment. You married but found no love there, so now you are having an affair. This is wrong, and you know it, but it just seems to be the best you can do.

One day you are with your lover in the secret place where you meet, and all of a sudden everything goes crazy! The door bursts open, men are dragging you from your bed, and without even giving you time to get dressed, they rush you out into the street, to the temple courtyard, and throw you in a heap at the feet of some judge for sentencing. Your humiliation is beyond words. You want to die. And you may get your wish, for the old law stipulates that an adultress can be taken outside the city and stoned until she is dead.

But what is going on? The judge is speaking to your accusers, not about *your* sins but about theirs! Then they begin to leave, until now only you and the judge remain. He stands up and looks right at you. He doesn't look at you as most men do—to lust after you; or to judge you (as do the religious ones); or to look right through you as if you weren't there (since you're "just" a woman). But his look contains concern, compassion, even pain over your humiliation. Somehow his look conveys dignity to you, even in this most undignified circumstance.

Finally the judge speaks: "Has no one condemned you?"

"No one, sir."

"Then neither do I. You may go." Words of grace and kindness, words you never expected to hear! But as you turn to leave, he adds, "Leave your sinful way of living." Words of guidance and concern.

Jesus spoke the *truth* to that woman that day: "Leave your life of sin." *You don't have to go on living this way,* he was saying to her; *your lifestyle is wrong.* He did not excuse or sugarcoat his words, as if to say, "Now, my dear, you're simply the victim of the new morality." No, the marriage vow is sacred, a pledge before God; to break it is sin.

But notice: he spoke the truth *in love.* He addressed her with respect and concern, while to the others she was nothing more than a pawn in their religious game. He extended grace to her when no one else would.

Did she change, become his follower? We don't know. The Bible does not say. But she never had a better chance to change than that day, when that man spoke the truth to her, in love.

Where Do Our Words Come From?

Where do words of honesty and love come from? Or for that matter, where do words of deceit and destruction come from? God's Word teaches that the primary communication organ is the *heart.* Not the lips or the tongue or the voice box, but the heart. Our Hero said so emphatically: ". . . For out of the overflow of the heart the mouth speaks. . . . For by your words you will be acquitted, and by your words you will be condemned" (Matt. 12:34b, 37, NIV).

In this Communication Age of ours, we need more than ever a speech teacher—one who can instruct us in the honest, loving use of those potent things called words. But even more fundamentally, we need a heart changer. All the speech courses and communication books in the world will not cleanse the human heart; only a redeemer can do that.

So we look to our Hero, God's finest communicator, his living Word to us (John 1:1–14). Jesus is the Speech Teacher par excellence, the only man who was ever totally honest and totally kind at the same time, all the time. But he is first of all the Redeemer, the Heart Changer, who wants to give us both the power and the grace we need to "speak the truth in love."

12

Heroic Forgiveness
Learning to Deal with Differences

Whenever we have first-time guests to our home, I like to lead them by a display case in my living room so I can say casually, "Oh, have you seen my ancient oil lamps from Israel?" Those ugly clay lamps may not fascinate all my guests, but they are treasures to me. Some are over two thousand years old and were giving light to some Jewish family about when and where a man named Jesus was first preaching the good news of God's love. Imagine that! Those old lamps help me remember that Jesus of Nazareth was just as real, just as touchable, as they are.

Today, two thousand years later, in our search for authentic heroes, we certainly want a hero who is real: not a product of media hype or comic-book imagination, but a genuine, flesh-and-blood hero. That is one good reason why this book is setting forth Jesus as the one true Hero for our time, and all time. *He was real.*

John opens his epistle with that very announcement. The One who is called "the Word of life," he writes—we have heard him, we have seen him with our own eyes, we have touched him with our hands (1 John 1:1). The unique claim that Christianity makes is that in Jesus Christ God himself took on flesh and blood and became one of us. The Creator

became one of his creatures, so we could touch him and
he us.

Rock Collecting

As we turn our attention in this chapter to the subject of
heroic forgiveness, I am thinking of something even older
than my ancient Israelite oil lamps—a big, round rock.

Dr. Carey Looney, a Christian counselor, has said that
many of us carry around with us what amounts to a sackful
of these. Each rock represents a bitter resentment, an unforgiven grudge, an unresolved conflict with the people in
our lives. We save them up in a sack, polished and ready, for
just the right moment.

Here's how it works. A husband and wife return home
from a party. Says she, "How could you say such a stupid
thing tonight? I was mortified!" (She's just lobbed a rock at
him.)

"Oh, yeah?" says he. "What about that air-head remark
you made at church on Sunday?" (Now he's reached down
inside his sack, and pulled out a retaliatory rock.)

"You're calling me an air-head," she says (as she goes into
her windup), "after what your mother said at the family
reunion last year?"

Not to be outdone, he pulls out the prize rock from his
collection, "Okay, you asked for it, what about the
time . . . ?"

And so it goes, until finally the battle is over, and they are
both emotionally exhausted and beaten. But they still have
enough energy to go around and pick up their rocks, wipe the
blood off them, and put them back in their sacks, ready for
the next round.

How would you feel, Dr. Looney asks, if you carried a
sackful of rocks around with you, all day, every day? The
answer, of course, is tired, very tired. And that is exactly how
unresolved conflict and unforgiven sins weigh on us.

Jesus understood that. You can hear his understanding in his great invitation: "Come to me, all you who are weary and burdened, and I will give you rest . . . rest for your souls" (Matt. 11:28–29, NIV). Without forgiveness, for ourselves and for others, our lives can be an exhausting, fatiguing succession of battles that are never won.

Jesus' Forgiveness Principle

So what does our Hero have to teach us about overcoming our inclination toward rock collecting? Jesus taught that there is a two-way "forgiveness principle" that begins with how God relates to us and then extends to how we relate to one another.

Once, Peter came to Jesus, wondering what the forgiveness quota is. Surely there's a limit, he was thinking. "Lord, how many times shall I forgive my brother when he sins against me? Up to seven times?" (Matt. 18:21, NIV). Now, the religious standard in that day seems to have been three times: forgive a man three times, then no more Mr. Nice Guy! So Peter may have been expecting Jesus' congratulations for his outstanding generosity.

But Jesus surprised Peter: "I tell you, not seven times but seventy-seven times" (v. 22, NIV). In other words, forgive him again and again and again. Then Jesus told a parable (vv. 23–35). "The kingdom of heaven is like this . . ." he began, meaning: where God rules, this is how it is.

There was once a man who owed his king ten thousand talents. Now, when Jesus threw out that figure, I'll bet someone in the audience that day gasped. Ten thousand talents was more like a national debt than an amount that one individual could owe. According to ancient records, that is equivalent to the tax revenue of all of ancient Palestine for twenty years!

The man says to the king, "I don't have the money. Be patient with me." Patient? Somebody probably laughed at that line. What is one man going to do to come up with that kind of money, kidnap the pharaoh of Egypt for ransom?

Then, incredibly, the king forgives him! Not an extension on the loan, with interest penalties, but a total clearing of the books! What does forgiveness like that feel like? How did you feel when you made the last payment on your car, or better, your house? Liberated! Unburdened! Set free! That is what forgiveness feels like. But the parable is not over.

The second incredible turn in Jesus' story comes when the king's servant, now relieved of his huge indebtedness, goes out and runs into a man who owes him a hundred denarii, pocket change by comparison. "Pay up!" he demands, grabbing him by the throat. "Be patient," the debtor gasps (sound familiar?). But he refused, Jesus tells us, and has him tossed in the local jail.

When the king hears about this, he is furious. "You scoundrel!" (NEB). "Couldn't you show the same kind of mercy to him that I showed to you?" In other words, "Didn't you learn anything from my mercy?" He tosses him into jail and reinstates his indebtedness.

That's the way it is where God rules, Jesus is saying—that is how the Father responds to our penitent pleas for his forgiveness, and that is how the Father responds to our small-heartedness when it comes to not forgiving others.

God's forgiveness has a condition, the Bible teaches:

"Blessed are the merciful, for they will be shown mercy" (Matt. 5:7, NIV).

"For if you forgive men when they sin against you, your heavenly Father will also forgive you. But if you do not forgive men their sins, your Father will not forgive your sins" (Matt. 6:14–15, NIV).

". . . judgment without mercy will be shown to anyone who has not been merciful . . ." (James 2:13, NIV).

Our Hero has provided us with at least two strong motivations for giving up our "rock collections," our stored-up anger and nonforgiving spirit. One is *the grateful heart.* The forgiving heart is an emancipated heart, liberated from bondage, because Jesus "paid a debt he did not owe, a debt I could not pay." Because of the cross, I have been, in the biblical term, "justified"—in Christ my slate is wiped clean, my record reads, "Not guilty."

The second motivation is *a sober recognition of the wrath of God.* As a justified child of God, I am saved from his wrath (Rom. 5:9). God's wrath is his holy displeasure with the sin that can twist the human spirit and ultimately separate us from him. Our God is rich in mercy and slow to anger (Ps. 145:8), but the Scriptures clearly teach he will show no mercy to the merciless. I do not want to be found outside the mercy of God.

Four Forgiveness Resolutions

When we encounter those annoying, anger-producing conflicts and differences with one another, it is so easy to reach down into our "sacks of rocks" and start filling the air with them. Here are four resolutions that can help us resist the temptation.

1. *I resolve not to be quarrelsome.* Proverbs, the ancient wisdom book of Israel, has nothing good to say about the person who constantly bickers and argues: "He who loves a quarrel loves sin . . ." (17:19, NIV). "It is to a man's honor to avoid strife, but every fool is quick to quarrel" (20:3, NIV). And "a quarrelsome wife is like a constant dripping on a rainy day" (27:15, NIV). Let me hasten to add that I know some pretty drippy husbands, too.

Quarreling is the resolution process stuck in neutral, going back over the same grueling grievances again and again. You can drain a marriage, or any other relationship, dry that way. When you find yourselves stuck in a bickering-and-nagging cycle, call it what it is: drippy quarrelsomeness. Then move on to resolution two:

2. *I resolve to accept **my** responsibility in our conflict.* Sometimes when I am teaching a communications seminar, I will ask people to repeat these words after me: "I was

wrong, and I'm sorry"—just to see if they do it, without spraining every muscle in their mouths and egos. Often a wife will turn to her husband, or vice versa, with a look that says, "Well, that's the first time in a while I've heard those words come out of *your* mouth!"

Do you feel that it is weak or undignified to confess your wrongs? Elton Trueblood says, "Seldom in a man's life is he actually nobler than when he says, 'I was wrong; I am ashamed; please forgive me'" *(The Lord's Prayers)*. He's right—it takes strength and nobility, not weakness and cowardice, to admit that you have been wrong. It is often the first step to healthy conflict resolution and forgiveness. James counsels us: "Therefore confess your sins to one another, and pray for one another . . ." (5:16).

3. *I resolve to accept you.* People are different. Have you noticed that? We usually marry someone different from ourselves, for good reason: they fill in our gaps, complement our gifts with their own. But in conflict situations we often find ourselves resenting those differences. "Why can't you see it my way?" we complain. Because they see it *their* way, their unique, individual way, that's why.

Writing to Christians in Rome, Paul counsels a very diverse fellowship to be more patient with each other's differences in lifestyle and religious upbringing. "Accept one another, then," he writes, "just as Christ accepted you, in order to bring praise to God" (Rom. 15:7, NIV). It is never right to tolerate evil or injustice, but it is right to be more tolerant of one another's individuality.

4. *I resolve to forgive you.* When all is said and done, I think of God's mercy towards me. I think of his attitude toward the unforgiving person. And I think of my Hero, who said through teeth clinched in the pain of death, of those who had put him on the cross, "Father, forgive them." The next time you are tempted to pick up a rock, remember our Hero, won't you?

13

Heroic Commitment
Making and Keeping the Marriage Promise

I keep a photo album of the couples whose wedding services I have performed over the years. Today, some are happily married; some are unhappily married; and some are no longer married at all.

On that very special day when the three of us stood together at the front of the church, all things seemed possible. Nothing could defeat their love for each other. Nothing could make them compromise their vow of devotion. But, for some of these couples and a million other couples this year, the wedding promise was a promise they could not or would not keep.

Is it possible to have a heroic marriage today? Is it possible to make a marriage promise that will last until death? I say it is—if you have chosen the right Hero, the One who can teach and empower you to make an unbreakable promise. No, Jesus never married, but he knew more about keeping promises that any man who ever lived.

Marital Honor and Purity

The Bible says, "Marriage should be honored by all, and the marriage bed kept pure . . ." (Heb. 13:4, NIV). God's will for marriage, captured in two old-fashioned words, is simply this: *honor* and *purity.*

First, the holy union of a man and a woman for life is something that should be held in high honor, even reverence. I once heard singer Linda Ronstadt explain why she never married: "I think marriage is something invented by human beings." Sorry, Linda, we must disagree. Marriage is *God's* idea.

In the very beginning, the Creator brought Adam and Eve to one another because, as he said, "It is not good that the man should be alone . . ." (Gen. 2:18). Before any other social institution, before governments, schools, armies, even churches, there was marriage, instituted by God at the dawn of history. Marriage is God's invention, not ours, and should be honored as such.

Second, the marriage bed should be "kept pure." This is God's clear call to sexual faithfulness. But our culture often does not make sexual faithfulness either easy or attractive, does it? Consider these cultural pressures:

1. *The Sexual Overstimulation of America.* Think about the obligatory bedroom scene that finds its way into so much TV—daytime, prime-time, late-time, any time—a scene that interestingly enough seldom pictures married persons with their own spouses. If you add to that the seductive ads and commercials, music and music videos, you might conclude that we Americans give thought to little else than the satisfaction of our hormonal urges.

2. *The Multiple-Choice Syndrome.* The voice of choice beckons to us: "If you don't like it, change it. Immediate gratification is your inalienable right!" (So I sit in front of the TV set with my little remote channel-changer and flip from station to station until my poor wife is ready to flip herself.)

In a multiple-choice society, we can begin to lose the will to make those irrevocable choices, to make a vow—like marriage—and stick with it. If we view marriage as disposable, like a used soda bottle, we will be quicker to change partners when the current one ceases to gratify us.

3. *The Easy-Divorce Myth.* This is the modern fiction that says that divorce is just not the big deal it once was, back in our repressed and unenlightened past. Dr. Joyce Brothers was quoted recently as saying that in the future we will have a more upbeat attitude toward divorce, play down the negatives, throw divorce showers, and give divorce gifts *(U.S. News and World Report).*

Yes, some legal aspects of divorce have been streamlined, but I seriously question that divorce is in any other sense "easier" today. My divorced friends have found nothing easy in divorce. Neither have their children. C. S. Lewis said it well when he wrote that divorce is "like cutting up a living body. . . . more like having both your legs cut off than it is like dissolving a business partnership" *(Mere Christianity).*

4. *Lots of Bad Advice.* Some would have us believe that sexual fidelity in marriage is just a very old and naive hang-up. Dr. Ruth Westheimer, the grandmotherly sex therapist, disarms us with her cuteness and then says, "If you can have a sparkling affair safely, so nobody will ever find out, do it. Have fun!" Such advice strikes me as the moral equivalent of handing a child a loaded gun.

I saw an article in the business section of a major newspaper entitled "Conduct Business Affairs Discreetly to Avoid Scandal." It cautioned against open interoffice affairs because they tend to hinder professional advancement. Not because they break trust or betray love or destroy families, but because they might keep you from getting a raise.

"But I Have Promises to Keep"

No, fidelity is not an easy promise to keep today. But it can be done, because marriage is God's idea, and he most of all wants to see marriages work as he intended from the beginning.

In his teaching, our Hero Jesus confirmed his Father's desire that marriage be for life. He quoted Genesis 2:24—"'For this reason a man will leave his father and mother and be united to his wife, and the two will become one flesh,'" and then he added, for emphasis, ". . . Therefore what God has joined together, let man not separate" (Matt. 19:5–6, NIV).

But what happens when a man at mid-life begins to feel that his youth is fleeting, his marriage stagnant? Or a woman experiences deep feelings of being unlovely and unappreciated? And a thousand secular voices join in chorus to whisper, "Do it. Don't be so inhibited. You're unfulfilled. Do something for yourself for a change!"

Why is it that people who "know better"—good people, church people—sometimes cheat on their marriage partners? Often, because of *feelings:* a nagging sense of infatuation or loneliness or boredom or taken-for-granted–ness. "This must be right," they say. "It feels right." But they have been victimized by their feelings, as Solomon described it long ago, "There is a way which seems right to a man, but its end is the way to death" (Prov. 14:12).

But, borrowing Robert Frost's familiar words, I have promises to keep! And if I am to keep my marriage promises, I need an internal defense system that is stronger than my feelings. I need a spiritual resolve that draws its strength from the very faithfulness of God himself.

The Covenant Promise

The Bible speaks of a commitment that is stronger than feelings, stronger than the seduction of culture, stronger than the gates of hell itself: it is "covenant." A covenant is a promise, a vow, a commitment of allegiance, a holy bond.

Covenant is what God made with the faithful old Bedouin, Abraham, and later with all Israel through that fiery deliverer, Moses. To Jeremiah the prophet, God revealed what he called "a new covenant," one that would be written on human hearts (Jer. 31:31–33). And when Jesus sat at the Last Supper, he raised a cup emblematic of his blood, about to be shed, and said, "This cup is the new covenant in my blood, which is poured out for you" (Luke 22:20, NIV). He would soon keep that promise.

What does that have to do with marriage today? Just this: God is a covenant God, a promise-keeping God. He sent his Son to spill his blood to seal that covenant. So, is *he* not the one to look to, to find the definition and motivation and power we need to make our marriage promises last?

If you are married, think back to a promise you once made. Someone asked you, "Do you take this one to be your wife [or husband], to live together according to God's Holy Word, and do you promise to love, honor, and cherish this one, both in sickness and in health, and do you promise that, forsaking all others, you will devote yourself to this one alone, as long as you both shall live?"

When you said, through trembling lips, "I do," that was a *covenant* vow you made, a holy commitment before God. If we are to bring permanence and excellence to marriage, we must let God teach us the meaning of that covenant.

How to Have a Covenant Marriage

1. You begin with a personal life-covenant to God's Son. One of God's loveliest qualities is his *faithfulness*. We are reminded of his promise: "'Never will I leave you; never will I forsake you'" (Heb. 13:5, NIV). In the same spirit his Son Jesus pledges, ". . . I am with you always, to the close of the age" (Matt. 28:20). With Jesus as your Lord and your Hero, you have the finest Teacher there is, from whom to learn the lessons of faithfulness and promise keeping.

2. Upon that foundation you can then begin to build an ongoing covenant commitment to your marriage partner. Jesus becomes Lord not only of your personal life but of your marriage as well.

I recently read of a British couple who had a fight and decided to divorce at their wedding reception! Your spouse needs to know that, in a throw-away society with disposable relationships, he or she is irreplaceable in your life: "I will never leave you." Not weary resignation ("I guess I'm stuck with you"), but an ever-fresh commitment to an ever-maturing marriage.

3. Renew that commitment every so often. Pull out that wrinkled wedding dress, rent a tux (probably with a more generous waistline than the original), and repeat those covenant promises to each other. You may just find that the years have given you a deeper understanding and appreciation for those vows—fresh meaning to words like "love," and "honor," and "cherish."

4. Finally, feed that commitment with communication. Marriage experts tell us with almost boring repetition that happy couples talk a lot. Reuel Howe says that communication is to love what blood is to our bodies: when the flow of blood stops, the body dies; when the flow of communication stops, love dies.

So open up. Share the big things and the little things. Make time for the intimate moments, verbal *and* physical. Every so often, say, "Honey, you know what I really appreciate about you. . . ." Then fill in the blank, as many times as you can.

Watch Out for Drift

There is an old gospel song whose chorus goes: "Come to Jesus today, he will show you the way./You're drifting too far from the shore."

That spiritual "drift" can happen in marriage as well as in other areas of spiritual accountability before God. Slowly, gradually, we make little choices that alter our values, shift our loyalties. Without meaning to, we substitute a secular model of marriage for a spiritual one. We find we are giving our best energy and creativity to our jobs. We become lazy at home, lazy at listening, lazy at loving. And the covenant is compromised. We have drifted away from each other and from a holy, sacred vow before God.

Marriage should be honored by all, and the marriage bed kept pure. May the God who invented marriage give us the power and the forgiveness necessary to bring covenant commitment back to our marriages. May we put into daily practice these good words from my friend Landon Saunders:

Marriage means a man and a woman looking deeply into one another's eyes and saying: "I will never leave you. Others may come and go in your life, but I never will. If you wrinkle, I will love you. If you fail, I will stay with you. If you get sick, I'll feed you, bathe you, sit up with you—anything—except leave you. I will never leave you" *(Heartbeat).*

14

Heroic Peace
Finding the Heart's Peace and Quiet

Everywhere you go these days you see someone with a portable tape player and earphones. I wear mine while I jog, to distract me from the pain. A friend of mine bought one to listen to on the commuter train into and out of New York City. The first day he used it, he noticed (a) that he wasn't getting very good sound quality, and (b) that the woman sitting next to him kept giving him strange looks as he tried to listen to his Willie Nelson tape. Later he found that he'd had the earphones turned out, instead of in.

We seem unable, even unwilling, to escape noise these days—tape players on our trains or as we jog, telephones in our cars, music in our elevators, TVs in every room of the house. We have grown so accustomed to noise that quiet makes us uncomfortable. We rush to fill any void of silence with more noise. And, yet, isn't it true that within each of us there is a deep inner yearning for silence, for peace and quiet? We long to find a place of central calm in the heart of the cyclone, to turn down the volume knob on this loud universe.

Did you know that noise is a major contributor to stress? Studies show, for instance, that people living and working near major airports tend to have higher rates of hypertension, heart disease, even suicide, than residents of quieter areas. (I wonder what studies show about the effects of kid-noise on us parents of three-year-olds!)

We hear the ancient words beckoning us, "Be still, and know that I am God . . ." (Ps. 46:10). But we have forgotten how to be still. If only someone could raise a hand over our lives, like Jesus did the stormy sea, and say, "Peace. Be still." Well, authentic peace and quiet may not come as quickly or dramatically to our noisy lives as it did that day long ago to the Sea of Galilee, but we can be looking in the right direction. As we are committed to doing in this series of studies, let us again "fix our eyes on Jesus, the author [the Pioneer, the Hero] and perfecter of our faith . . ." (Heb. 12:2, NIV).

Beware the Noisy Heart

As much as the noise outside us affects us, a more crucial issue concerns the noise *inside* us. Whatever may be going on around you, do you have an internal peace and quiet? People can live a fairly unstressed lifestyle and still not be at at peace within themselves.

Wayne Oates, a counselor and teacher of counselors, has written a helpful book with an intriguing title: *Nurturing Silence in a Noisy Heart*. Do you have a "noisy heart"? A noisy heart can be that of a very busy person, a heart that has gotten overloaded with too many facts, figures, and feelings. The din of all those messages—all so urgent, so insistent—can drown out life's gentle, healing sounds and leave us empty. An old saying warns, "Beware the barrenness of a busy life."

Often a noisy heart is one that echoes with soul-grieving sounds: the tones of discord, rage, frustration, painful mem-ories, unforgiven sins. It is interesting that our language gives us many idioms to describe what happens if our heart noises are not quieted. At the least, we get heartburn. At the worst, we become hardhearted. Or heartless. Or we lose heart. Or we suffer a broken heart.

An ancient biblical proverb says, "Above all else, guard your heart, for it is the wellspring of life" (Prov. 4:23, NIV). Guard your heart. Do not neglect its care. Tend it well, because it is the fountainhead, the freshwater source, the wellspring, from which your life flows. Who you are "at heart" is the man or woman God sees. "A man is what he is before God," a wise man once said, "and nothing else."

Maybe if we had lived in ancient Israel, or in a "Little House on the Prairie," peace and quiet would have been easier to find. Who knows? The fact remains that most of us live noisy, busy lives here and now. So where do we go to find our heart's peace and quiet?

Where Jesus Found Peace

Look at Jesus. His was a calm and peaceful spirit; and yet his adult life, I think most would agree, was a pretty noisy and stressful one. See if you can picture this scene from the Gospel of Mark:

> . . . because so many people were coming and going that they [Jesus and the apostles] did not even have a chance to eat, he said to them, "Come with me by yourselves to a quiet place and get some rest." So they went away by themselves in a boat to a solitary place. But many who saw them leaving recognized them and ran on foot from all the towns and got there ahead of them. When Jesus landed and saw a large crowd, he had compassion on them . . . (Mark 6:31–34, NIV).

After Jesus fed this hungry crowd of five thousand, Mark says, "he went into the hills to pray" (v. 46). Clearly, here is a picture of a man struggling—both for himself and his friends—to keep a healthy balance between meeting the needs of people and meeting his own spiritual and emotional needs. How did he manage to do it? How did Jesus nurture peace and quiet in his noisy life?

1. *Jesus found peace and quiet in* **solitude.** He made *time* and *space* for peace in his busy life. "Let's get away to a quiet

place for some rest," he told his apostles. But the crowds ambushed him at the pass! He sailed off to what he thought was a solitary place, but when he arrived, there they were, sitting there waiting for him with big smiles on their faces.

But other times he did manage to get away for those essential quiet moments. Mark tells us elsewhere, "Very early in the morning, while it was still dark, Jesus got up, left the house and went off to a solitary place, where he prayed" (Mark 1:35, NIV). Often he withdrew into wilderness places. Why? To get away from people. But why? So he could come *back* to people, refreshed, reoriented, to serve and love them again.

Quiet will not just happen for most of us; we have to make it a spiritual priority. Not so long ago, I made an exciting discovery: I can take my phone off the hook! There is no law against it, though I guess I used to think there was. Another discovery: I can sit in a room with a TV, and not have to turn it on. No law! I know of a family that designated a "quiet chair" in their house. Whoever is sitting in that chair is to be left alone. Do whatever it takes to make time and space for quiet.

2. *Jesus found peace and quiet in* **prayer.** That's what he usually did in those quiet places, talked to and *listened* to his Father. Who better than the Father to help us sort through all the confusing and discordant sounds in our noisy hearts? There is an old hymn that goes, "There is a place of quiet rest, near to the heart of God."

They marveled at Jesus' calm and composure during his trial and execution. Isaiah prophesied that it would be so: "He was oppressed and afflicted, yet he did not open his mouth; and as a sheep before her shearers is silent, so he did not open his mouth" (Isa. 53:7, NIV). Where did that quiet confidence come from? I believe that much of it came from Gethsemane, where Jesus had wrestled with his fears in prayer before the Father and determined once and for all, "Not my will, but thine be done" (Luke 22:42b).

But I believe prayer is more than closing your eyes and talking. It is also opening your eyes and reading God's Word—and listening. It is opening your heart to his presence—and listening. "Be still," says God—hush, now—"and know that I am God" (Ps. 46:10b). In the quietness of prayer, Catherine Doherty says, we are free to "listen to God's speech in his wondrous, terrible, gentle, loving, all-embracing silence."

3. *Jesus found peace and quiet in* **forgiveness.** So much of the noise in our hearts comes from our insistence on carrying around with us a whole collection of grudges and guilts—sins we refuse to forgive others for, sins we refuse to confess to ourselves and God. What a racket they cause in our hearts!

In a powerful documentary film, *Shoah,* a man named Simon Srebnik, a Polish Holocaust survivor, looks over a quiet field that once was the Nazi concentration camp at Chelmno, and says:

> I can't believe I'm here. . . . It was always this peaceful here. Always. When they burned two thousand people—Jews—every day, it was just as peaceful. No one shouted. Everyone went about his work. It was silent. Peaceful. Just as it is now.

As much as we all yearn for a little quiet, we need more than quiet, for quiet can mask a silent, internal cancer. In a "cold war," there may be no battles, but there is still warfare. There are cold-war nations, and there are cold-war marriages and families and individual lives: peaceful-looking outside, a war raging inside.

God's forgiveness brings quiet where there was accusation, peace where there was war. Amidst the noises of hate and brutality at Golgotha that day, there was one man secure enough in the peace of God to say, "Father, forgive them."

4. Finally, *Jesus found peace and quiet in his one clear* **commitment**—to be *God's man.* There was much noise—

joyful noise—that day when Jesus came riding into Jerusalem to shouts of "Hosanna! The King is coming!" And here he came, the King on a donkey, entering the city as the Prince of Peace. But he knew that the moods of crowds change, and soon they would be making a different noise: "Crucify him!" But whether the noise outside him was "Hosanna!" or "Crucify!" I believe this Prince had peace in his heart because, therein, he had that one magnificent obsession—his one clear commitment, to be God's man.

Kierkegaard said, "Purity of heart is to will one thing." Above the noise in our hearts, our ears must be attuned to that one voice, the voice of the Prince whose kingdom we seek first, the Hero we have decided to follow, wherever he leads. For without the Prince, there is no real peace.

The true peace and quiet rests gently in the heart of a person reconciled to his God through Christ. "Therefore, since we are justified by faith, we have peace with God through our Lord Jesus Christ" (Rom. 5:1). Justified. Forgiven. At rest. Secure. The Prince brings peace to the noisy heart.

15

Heroic Vocation
Discerning Your Life's Calling

As I thumb through my old baseball cards, today's cardboard equivalent of precious metals, I see not only investment potential but heroic images of my youth: Willie Mays, Ted Williams, Hank Aaron—my boyhood heroes. But then I come to one special card from 1959, now somewhat worn despite loving care. Here was the biggest hero of them all, when I was eleven: Mickey Mantle, center fielder for the New York Yankees. He had the arms of a blacksmith and could run like a deer. Once, he almost hit a ball out of old Yankee Stadium! "The Mick" was a figure of heroic proportions.

But when I became a man, I put away childish things (except for some of those baseball cards). I needed a man's hero, not a boy's. As we consider heroes and heroic living, let me identify for you my Hero for the rest of my life—Jesus of Nazareth.

In the New Testament Book of Hebrews, Jesus is described with one of the great "hero words" of the ancient world, the *Archegos*. He is our Pioneer, the Bible says, the One who has gone before us to show us how life can be lived to heroic proportions:

119

. . . let us run with perseverance the race that is set before us, looking to Jesus the pioneer and perfecter of our faith, who for the joy that was set before him endured the cross, despising the shame, and is seated at the right hand of the throne of God (Heb. 12:1b–2).

Redefining Our Dreams

My earliest dream was to play center field for the Yankees. As a kid I would listen to their games on radio, living out the drama of every pitch. And when Mickey Mantle put one in the upper deck, it was I who rounded the bases, touching each one carefully, then tipping my cap with modesty and dignity to the fans. I have been forced to give up that fantasy, reluctantly; the Yankees just aren't interested in thirty-nine-year-old rookies who can't hit a curve . . . or a fast ball . . . or a changeup.

There comes to each of us the realization, sometimes painful, that many of our dreams will never be more than just that. I will never play center field for the Yankees. I will never be a leading man on Broadway. I will never write the great American novel. I will never be President of the United States.

Our dreams, like our heroes, have to be redefined along the way. The realities of the adult world force us to exchange romantic fantasy for the real facts. We face those realities when we finally have to answer that weighty question: "What are you going to be when you grow up?"

Sometimes the redefinition of dreams happens again in mid-life or even later. Circumstances outside our control force a mid-course vocational correction. The closing of a factory. A crippling accident. The death of a spouse. Mandatory retirement. Careers and dreams must be reconsidered.

We may have to reassess our dreams because our lives and work have just gotten stuck in neutral. We have to redefine what we are doing before we bore ourselves to death.

Kierkegaard said, "Boredom is the root of all evil." He makes a powerful point. What is emptier than the heart of a person playing the lead role in a life going nowhere? Locked into a stifling routine, day following day—finding no joy or purpose in his or her work, relationships, or religion. That's what someone has called "terminal boredom."

I live just outside New York City now (not too far from Yankee Stadium). Folks around New York like to talk about "life in the fast lane." And it is—fast-paced, hard-pushing—rush, scurry, dash, hurry! I see people looking at their watches as if they had time bombs strapped to their wrists! But some of the busiest people I know are some of the most *bored* people I know. Their lives are not fulfilled; they are just filled.

Nobody sets out to live a small life. But that is exactly what we can end up with, if we follow the wrong heroes or buy into small, meager ambitions. Where do you go to find a magnificent ambition, one that is big and heroic and never boring?

A Vocation from God

Jesus was always calling people to big ambitions and dreams: "But seek ye first the Kingdom of God . . ." (Matt. 6:33, KJV). Now that's big! Discover life under the sovereign reign of Almighty God, Jesus urges us. Make that your life's quest, your consuming passion.

Or how about this challenge: "Deny yourself, take up your cross, and follow me" (cf. Mark 8:34). "Lay aside the trivial and selfish ambitions," he is saying, "and follow me to glory. Let me be your hero and guide. I'll not lead you wrong. I'll give you a noble work to do." Jesus makes the ambitions of modern power-brokers and entrepreneurs look paltry by comparison!

Look carefully at that word *vocation*. In the New Testament, the word *(klesis)* sometimes translated "vocation" is usually translated "calling." In Ephesians 4:1, Paul writes,

". . . I urge you to live a life worthy of the calling [vocation] you have received" (NIV). What kind of "calling" is that? The calling to be a preacher? No, Paul is talking about God's calling of every Christian into the family of believers, the church (cf. Eph. 3:15, 21).

Today, we commonly use "vocation" to mean a person's job or career. And a "calling" is often thought of as some semi-mystical experience that only preacher-types have. But God's Word says clearly that, in Christ, *every* man and woman has a calling, a vocation, a ministry, a unique work to do: "You are a chosen people," Peter says, "a royal priesthood [that means every Christian] . . . a people belonging to God" (1 Peter 2:9a, NIV).

In John's Gospel there is a wonderful story about a man who had a pretty small life until Jesus gave it new dimension and destiny. The disciples noticed a blind man, and decided to discuss him: "Rabbi, who sinned, this man or his parents, that he was born blind?"—"Neither this man nor his parents sinned," replied Jesus, "but this happened so that the work of God might be displayed in his life" (John 9:2–3, NIV).

Here is a man whom most of society had written off as useless, unproductive. But Jesus was saying, "Let me tell you about this guy—he may not look like much to you, but his life is about to become a display model *for the work of God.*"

And just before he gives this man his sight, Jesus gives them—and us—one of the clearest and most challenging statements about vocation ever made: "As long as it is day, *we must do the work of him who sent me.* Night is coming, when no man can work" (John 9:4, NIV [italics mine]).

What is "the work" of God? I believe that, in a word, the work of God is *people.* The loving of people. The saving of people. The shaping of healthy, productive people. That's what God does. "For God so loved [who?] the world [people] that he gave his one and only Son. . ." (John 3:16, NIV). Gave his very best, and to whom? To people. The work of God was, and is, people. In Christ he even became one of his people.

What, then, is "the work of people"? *To do the work of God.* "As long as it is day, we must do the work of him who sent [Jesus]." We do God's work by loving and serving people.

Are Your Dreams Big Enough?

How about your vocational dreams—are they big enough? Do you have a mission, or just a job? A calling, or merely a career? I'd like you to ask yourself four questions about your vocational values:

1. *What is my work dedicated to?* Sometimes you hear of a ballplayer "dedicating" a season to the memory of someone he loves; his dedication presumably motivates him to greater performance. But dedication in and of itself is not necessarily noble. I know of some pretty dedicated, hard-working crooks! Our lives are only as noble and as heroic as the object of our dedication.

"Whatever you do," Paul wrote, "work at it with all your heart, as working *for the Lord,* not for men" (Col. 3:23, NIV [italics mine]). If it is God that you dedicate your work to, God whose call you answer each day, then you have not only a job, but a true vocation.

2. *What's more important in the big picture—what I do, or who I am?* When you say to someone, "Tell me about yourself," how do they typically answer? By telling you their job, what they *do* (especially men): "I'm a sprocket salesman with Acme Sprockets, Inc."

But "who I am" is much more important than "what I do." Randy Becton has put it this way: when you are confined to a hospital bed for twelve weeks, and you can't "produce," you are still who you are. When you have been laid off from the only company you ever worked for, you are still who you are. When you have turned sixty-five, and you have more know-how than ever before, but it's mandatory retirement time, you are still who you are.

That is why it is essential that you have your primary calling secure: in Christ you are part of the family of God, and nothing can touch that.

3. *What will my great-grandchildren know of me?* What legacy of spirit and memory and faith will I leave behind? How will I be remembered on those nights after I'm gone, when the family gets out that shoebox of old pictures, and starts to reminisce? Will they say, "Ah, Great-Grandpa, now there was a man who loved people, who helped his neighbor, who made a difference"? Will they say, "His work was people, and he did good work"?

William James wrote, "The great use of life is to spend it for something that will outlast it." Bear this in mind: nothing will outlast the work of the eternal kingdom of God.

4. *Am I working at something that no circumstance can defeat, and that even death cannot rob me of?* Do you remember the sad Olympics experience of Mary Decker Slaney, the great women's distance runner? For years she worked and sacrificed and trained, only to be tripped—accidentally—in the 1984 Olympics final by a barefoot British teenager.

I don't know what other dreams Mary Decker Slaney has. But I do know this: I don't want my life's greatest ambition to be something that a bare foot can ruin. Jobwise, I may someday be fired, become disabled, or be retired. But if my calling is from God, then no mere circumstance will be able to stop my greatest "work." And death—death will be but the final promotion.

Thomas Carlyle said, "Blessed is he who has found his work." God has issued a calling to every man and woman who will hear him. This is not a mysterious voice in the night. It is the calling to be his children, to follow his Son, to do his work. If ever there was a heroic calling, this is it!

Let us give ear to those compelling words from Jesus, bright words but with a hint of shadow over them: "We must work the works of him who sent me, while it is day; night comes, when no one can work" (John 9:4).

16

Heroic Vulnerability
Developing Deeper Relationships

Junk mail. How many noble trees are being needlessly sacrificed so that our mailboxes can be stuffed with that unsolicited, unwanted stuff? It's not all worthless, though. Some pieces are downright entertaining, thanks to the confused computers that generate them. A local bank sincerely solicits my business but greets me as "Den Durham." A sales brochure sent to my office at the Church of Christ begins, "Dear Chris Church. . . ." Another starts off, "Dear Mr. Church of Christ" (for a moment I thought I'd won an award). One mailing list sends me junk mail addressed to the "Church of the Hily Sprit" (meant to be "Holy Spirit," I suppose).

But I am more perturbed than amused when I receive a piece of junk mail from a computer that warmly begins, "Dear friend. . . ." Neither this mail-order house, nor their direct-mail marketing division, yea, nor their cordial computer, has the right to address me as "friend."

We get a lot of slightly inhuman messages, don't we? The bored teenage checkout girl at the local grocery recites automatically, "Have a nice day." A bumper sticker with a happy

Material in this chapter was adapted from my book, *Speaking from the Heart* © 1986, Sweet Publishing Co., Ft. Worth, TX.

face instructs us, "Smile, God loves you." Or a faded, peeling sign off to one side of the road reads, "Jesus Saves."

Why do those messages leave us feeling cold and empty, however true or pleasant-sounding the words? What's missing? The human touch is missing. The warm, heart-felt, heart-healing personal contact that we all need.

In the Genesis account of the creation of the world, do you remember what God keeps saying as he evaluates his work? "It is good," he says again and again. (I like Bill Cosby's observation: "Man constructs a car and calls it 'Awesome!'; God creates a tree and calls it 'Good.'") But then God abruptly pronounces something "*not* good." What was it? It was man, Adam, alone. "It is not good that the man should be alone . . ." declares God (Gen. 2:18). With those words the Creator revealed a fundamental fact about his creatures.

We need *relationships*—not superficial acquaintances, but real, honest, trusting relationships—if we are to be what God created us to be. But how do you make and keep a real realtionship? In search of an answer, let us again use Jesus as our mentor and model, our teacher and example. Jesus, you will see as you read through the Gospels, had this wonderful way of getting beneath the surface with people, of communicating with them about more than just "news, weather, and sports."

The Risk of Vulnerability

If you find that most of your relationships never get much deeper than news, weather, and sports, it may be fear that is holding you back—fear of being hurt or unaccepted by others because you have made yourself vulnerable to them.

Lately a new word from the Soviet Union has appeared on the front page: *glasnost*. It means "openness" and supposedly signals a new governmental policy of candor and freedom of expression in the USSR. But it seems that the Soviet people are not altogether comfortable with the new *glasnost*. "How open can we be?" they wonder. How do you "open up" after so many generations of guardedness and secrecy? And what happens if the government returns to its old policy and prosecutes those who have been practicing the new openness? With *glasnost* comes vulnerability!

Vulnerability is by definition a risky proposition. "Vulnerable" means woundable, open or exposed to injury. Superman is "invulnerable"; you can't hurt him. But we are not supermen or superwomen; we can be hurt, and hurt deeply.

But the problem is, vulnerability is a price we pay for the precious privilege of loving. To love others is to make yourself vulnerable to them, woundable by them. It is a risk, an adventure, a leap of faith. C. S. Lewis has said that to love at all is to be vulnerable, and the only sure way to make certain that your heart will never be bruised or broken is never to give it to anyone. You can wrap it up safe in a coffin of selfishness, he says, but there it will become hard, unbreakable, and irredeemable. "The only place outside Heaven where you can be perfectly safe from all the dangers . . . of love," writes Lewis, "is Hell" *(The Four Loves)*.

The Ultimate Vulnerability

One of the most profound truths I have discovered in the New Testament is this: *Jesus is God made vulnerable to us.* Paul has given magnificent testimony to this fact:

> . . . being in very nature God, [Christ] did not count equality with God something to be grasped, but made himself nothing, taking the very nature of a servant, being made in human likeness. And being found in appearance as a man, he humbled himself and became obedient to death—even death on a cross! (Phil. 2:6–8, NIV).

Here is the ultimate love, the ultimate vulnerability— God taking on flesh, becoming one of us, exposing himself to all the wounds of being human, and finally submitting to the ugliest death imaginable, for our sake. Generations before, Isaiah had prophesied that our Messiah would be "wounded for our transgressions" (Isa. 53:5). He came to us woundable, and for our sins he was wounded.

God made himself vulnerable to us in Jesus Christ. We should not be surprised, then, to see Jesus communicating a special kind of openness to people as he built relationships with them. People did not lay down their lives for him simply because he was charismatic and interesting; it had more to do with the fact that he was compassionate and interested.

What is the shortest verse in the Bible? "Jesus wept" (John 11:35). It is also one of the most important, because it tells us that when God was one of us, he was open and vulnerable with us: he cried at gravesides, rejoiced at weddings, cradled babies in his arms, touched the untouchables. God touched us and let us touch him.

Here's a delightful study project. Choose one of the four Gospels and read through it, watching Jesus relate to others. Notice his wonderful way of communicating to people. He was saying things like: "Now, you're somebody I'd like to get to know." "How about a dinner invitation, Zacchaeus?" (Luke 19:5). "You impress me as a man of integrity, Nathanael" (John 1:47). "I have a nickname for you, Simon—I'll call you 'Rock'" (Matt. 16:18). Wouldn't you be drawn to someone who showed that kind of sincere personal interest in you?

From the Shallows to the Depths

In John 4 we find one of the lengthiest accounts of a conversation Jesus had with one individual. Study it carefully and you will see a conversation moving from the shallows to the depths. A Samaritan woman comes to the local well to draw water, as she had likely done a thousand times before. But this trip will change her life. She is startled to hear a male voice ask, "Will you give me a drink?" (4:7, NIV).

1. Jesus *notices* her. First, we must "tune in" to people if we are to have any chance of relating to them. Jesus really saw people; that is, he paid careful attention to those around him. Seeing people is the first step to relationship.

2. Jesus *accepts* her as worthy of conversation. In his culture, a proper Jewish gentleman just did not speak publically to a Samaritan, or to a person with a sinful reputation, or to a woman. And this lady was all three! But rather than categorize her—"Samaritan," "sinner," "woman"—he sees a uniquely precious human being.

3. Jesus asks her for *help*. "Will you give me a drink?" He knew that people like to help people, when they are able. Even in New York City, I have never failed to get help with directions when I needed it, if I looked bewildered long enough. Jesus let other people serve him.

4. Jesus talks about what is *relevant* to her. He begins with water, a basic human need; but as they talk, he moves to an even deeper human need. "Everyone who drinks this water will be thirsty again, but whoever drinks the water I give him will never thirst . . ." (4:13, NIV). Jesus talked about what was interesting and important to her.

5. Jesus keeps the conversation at a *personal* level. When talk turns to her five marriages, the woman begins to shift ground to an impersonal issue. She raises a current religious question about where to worship God acceptably (4:19–20). But Jesus draws it back to a personal issue: *how* to worship God acceptably, in spirit and in truth (vv. 23–24).

6. Jesus reveals his true *identity* to her. "I know that Messiah (called Christ) is coming," the woman says (4:25a, NIV). "I who speak to you," declares Jesus, "am he" (v. 26). What if we reveal to someone who we really are—what we feel, what we dream, what our faith is in—and they ignore it, or reject it, or laugh at it? Jesus took that risk. He disclosed himself to others.

That conversation should never have taken place, according to the social and religious rules of that day. But Jesus saw that women, prized her, asked her to serve him, talked about her needs and kept the conversation there, and opened up himself to her. And her life was never the same again.

Opening Up

There is a risk in being open to others. I would never counsel anyone to take that risk unless they have an anchor for their lives, a confidence in the unshakable love of God. Another word for that confidence is "faith." You see, if God loves and accepts me as I am, and he is changing me into something better, then my self-worth is firmly secured. If you were to reject me, I would be disappointed, sure, but not devastated. "If God is *for us*, who can be against us?" (Rom. 8:31, NIV [italics mine]).

Here are a few practical suggestions for getting beneath the surface with others:

1. Encourage people to talk about what they are interested in. Work on your listening. Interested people are perceived as interesting people.

2. Learn people's names, and remember them. My name is an important part of who I am (so I don't like being called "Den Durham" or "Chris Church").

3. Create good opportunities and environments for open conversation. "How about a cup of coffee?" "Care to join me for a walk?"

4. Always keep a confidence. Never, never gossip. Or people will quickly decide never to be open with you again.

5. Don't be consistently negative and argumentative. That could be the reason people won't spend very long in conversation with you.

6. Don't wear a mask with people—admit your faults, needs, and fears. This is not weakness. And it's not "unspiritual," either. If you don't believe me, read the writings of David, Jeremiah, and Paul.

7. Finally, plant yourself in a church where you can be open and vulnerable to people, as you are learning to trust and obey God. If it is a fellowship where Christ is truly Lord, you should find his kind of acceptance and encouragement and love right there.